Coleridge in William Greswell's Workbook

Reproduced by kind permission of the Syndics of Cambridge University Library
(Image Order Reference: DCU-3299)

J. C. C. Mays

Coleridge in William Greswell's Workbook

palgrave
macmillan

J. C. C. Mays
Department of English
University College
Dublin 4, Ireland

ISBN 978-3-031-38592-6   ISBN 978-3-031-38593-3   (eBook)
https://doi.org/10.1007/978-3-031-38593-3

© The Editor(s) (if applicable) and The Author(s), under exclusive licence to Springer Nature Switzerland AG 2023
This work is subject to copyright. All rights are solely and exclusively licensed by the Publisher, whether the whole or part of the material is concerned, specifically the rights of translation, reprinting, reuse of illustrations, recitation, broadcasting, reproduction on microfilms or in any other physical way, and transmission or information storage and retrieval, electronic adaptation, computer software, or by similar or dissimilar methodology now known or hereafter developed.
The use of general descriptive names, registered names, trademarks, service marks, etc. in this publication does not imply, even in the absence of a specific statement, that such names are exempt from the relevant protective laws and regulations and therefore free for general use.
The publisher, the authors, and the editors are safe to assume that the advice and information in this book are believed to be true and accurate at the date of publication. Neither the publisher nor the authors or the editors give a warranty, expressed or implied, with respect to the material contained herein or for any errors or omissions that may have been made. The publisher remains neutral with regard to jurisdictional claims in published maps and institutional affiliations.

Cover pattern © Melisa Hasan

This Palgrave Macmillan imprint is published by the registered company Springer Nature Switzerland AG.
The registered company address is: Gewerbestrasse 11, 6330 Cham, Switzerland

Paper in this product is recyclable.

PREFACE

This is, first of all, the story of a lost book found and read again. The book is unique: a bulky, hand-made late Victorian construct of sixty previously published essays and notices concerning Samuel Taylor Coleridge, published across ninety years and bound together before the end of the nineteenth century. There is nothing so comprehensive, even among twentieth-century compilations. The periodicals and extracts are drawn from English and American sources and extend from one to fifty-five pages. They encompass varying judgements on all branches of his career: poetry, talk, lectures, published essays and books of every sort. The compilation was evidently constructed with deliberate purpose, although that purpose is difficult to determine. It would seem primarily to test Coleridge's authority as a spiritual guide, although many other features of his work are taken into account. It would also seem that the compiler's decision was primarily negative—that he presented Coleridge's example as one implicitly not to be followed—and that this feature in particular is connected with how Carlyle's damning description in his *Life of Sterling* (1851) was received and applied, even many decades later.

At the same time—and this touches on the uniqueness of the book—there are undeniable connections made with figures who found something more positive in Coleridge's writing: who felt and proclaimed the attractions of his poetry, whose thinking was nourished by what the majority condemned as unsound, and which in the end coincided with what one of the most adventurous of nineteenth-century nonconformists had

v

vi PREFACE

argued—unheard at the time. This opposing strain of thought was rejected by the compiler, and there is no way of knowing if Coleridge—author of *Church and State*, the single title never explicitly discussed in the collection of reviews—would have gone so far as James Martineau. Meanwhile, the coincidence that connects with what is now called an ethics of "agent-based" virtue is revelatory. It opens a new chapter in the history of Coleridge's influence that has received little attention thus far. My conclusion on his present standing is downbeat. It has to be, but I hope I am wrong.

It is meanwhile important to remember that what I say of the man who constructed this unique compilation—William Greswell—is based almost solely on published sources and is therefore subject to revision with respect to his feelings. I mean, his book exists but what he left behind at some points remains unclear. In particular, I have not consulted the Greswell family concerning their memories, nor any remaining papers that may be in their possession. Nor have I consulted all the unpublished records, such as I know exist in Somerset, Oxford, Cambridge, London and South African repositories. I leave that task to Greswell's biographer, if the time ever comes, and I have concentrated on the Coleridge book he constructed: its contents and its significance. And I pause to mention that the unique Greswell compilation, along with books by and connected with Greswell—and indeed, all the materials connected with my Collected Coleridge contribution, and more—can now be consulted at the University of Limerick Library in Ireland.

A full complement of footnotes is not included because they would swamp the text: Greswell allowed his name to be misspelled in 1889 when he had his photograph taken, and what is there to explain except haste? However, I have added comments to many of the titles listed in the Bibliography, which will help explain where facts and ideas come from and where they might be pursued further.

I thank my wife Marianne, as ever, for her cheerful support and generous assistance: "without whom" and no less as we grow old. I should also like to thank John Cardwell and Cambridge University Library for the picture of Greswell that serves as a frontispiece; Brittany Bratcher and the Harry Ransom Center at the University of Texas, Austin, for supplying scans; Somerset Archives and Local Studies at Somerset Heritage Centre, Norton Fitzwarren, especially Harriet Moffett, for making a copy of

Greswell's list of books; Howard Dykes, Stock Librarian at Bristol Central Libraries, for his informed comments on nineteenth-century library stamps; and, finally, Marika Lysandrou and Esther Rani V for all their advice, patience and real help with the technology of Springer Nature.

Wicklow, Ireland   Jim Mays

Contents

1	Introduction	1
2	The Book-Object	7
3	The Way In	35
4	The Contents as They Stand	45
5	Greswell the Compiler	63
6	The Unwritten Script	75
7	Greswell After Coleridge	87
8	A Brave Conclusion	95
	Selected Greswell Bibliography	107
	Index	129

LIST OF ILLUSTRATIONS

Illustration 2.1	The imposing, carefully constructed volume which is the subject of this book	9
Illustration 2.2	A watermark on the flyleaf reveals the date when, or soon after, the book was constructed	10
Illustration 2.3	The top and side of pages were once trimmed level, while the lower side remains less regular	12
Illustration 2.4	Some extracts are already headed with full particulars	12
Illustration 2.5	Another example of the same	13
Illustration 2.6	Others have their source added in blue pencil	13
Illustration 2.7	Or added in black pencil. Not all the attributions are correct	14
Illustration 2.8	This ascription—in black pencil with a question mark—is the first of three references to the same magazine published in the United States. Here it is correct	15
Illustration 2.9	But this ascription—in blue pencil—has confused the American magazine with a British periodical. (It was not the London *Christian Reformer*)	15
Illustration 2.10	A second, similar mistake in muddling an English source with an American one	16
Illustration 2.11	Here, the periodical extract is cut and pasted onto wove paper	17
Illustration 2.12	The same again, the paper perhaps from an earlier family source	17
Illustration 2.13	This paste-up on Dodington Rectory paper—the imprint just visible here at top-right	19

xii LIST OF ILLUSTRATIONS

Illustration 2.14	Here the paper carries a blind stamp of a Manchester firm that went bankrupt more than twenty years before the essay pasted to it was printed	20
Illustration 2.15	And here the partly erased Bristol Library stamp shows the source-periodical was borrowed in the 1860s	21
Illustration 2.16	The first of the two contents pages, with blanks that show significant uncertainty concerning the source of some items as well as other confusions	22
Illustration 2.17	The second contents page. Note that someone has pencilled in the number of pages in the whole	23
Illustration 2.18	The top portion of a page of James Martineau's essay, with five-minute pencilled indications of how carefully it was studied	26
Illustration 2.19	Four similar markings on the review of Traill's book, which leave one wondering where the person who made them stands	27
Illustration 2.20	The author's instruction to the binder: to begin the collection at this point, leaving the previous six pages to be inserted later	28
Illustration 2.21	The inserted pencil number 24 keeps this essay by Joseph Sortain here, in this place, separate from the two other reviews of Coleridge's *Poetical Works* (1834)	30
Illustration 2.22	James Martineau's essay, with corrected numerals that reveal the care (and uncertainty) with which it was placed in the central position	31
Illustration 2.23	The details of Mozley's essay also corrected, showing the care with which its proper source was pursued	32
Illustration 2.24	The head of the page that contains Mozley's essay, with the illegible number or letter that again displays concern and uncertainty as to where the essay should be placed	32

CHAPTER 1

Introduction

Abstract I purchased a collection of nineteenth-century periodical reviews and essays on Coleridge on spec in 2016. It contain sixty such pieces, the latest of them dating from 1885, and as I became more familiar with them, my curiosity in the book as a whole grew. It gradually dawned on me that it must have been constructed by William Greswell (1848–1923), a Somersetshire clergyman at the beginning of his career, as he pondered whether to take orders. He afterwards put his collection together in a way that explains why he turned away from Coleridge, even while he left behind traces of what he found so attractive in Coleridge's thinking. After graduating from Oxford, he went to South Africa to teach and returned to become a member of the Royal Colonial Institute and write on aspects of colonial federation; and then again differently, as his first-hand knowledge became outdated from 1903 onwards, on local history. He also assisted Henry Nelson Coleridge gather support for the acquisition of the Coleridge Cottage in Nether Stowey, and died exactly a century ago. At the same time, what he found so attractive in Coleridge, despite his deep suspicion of it, intrigued me because it suggested a side of Coleridge that has not been sufficiently admitted up to now.

Keywords William Greswell summary • His life • His interests • His project • His book's peculiar importance

© The Author(s), under exclusive license to Springer Nature Switzerland AG 2023
J. C. C. Mays, *Coleridge in William Greswell's Workbook*, https://doi.org/10.1007/978-3-031-38593-3_1

1

In December 2016, I bought a book from Alex Alec-Smith, from whom I had bought many books in the past. She described it as a bound collection of separately printed essays and reviews, extracted from nineteenth-century sources, covering the full range of Coleridge's work, many of them unusual and difficult to find. They turned out to fill a volume with slightly smaller covers than the Bollingen Coleridge series but bulkier: with more pages than *Aids to Reflection* although slimmer than *Marginalia* volume 2. Although the volume does not incorporate excerpts from monographs or collections of essays—only from journals and newspapers—it adds up to the most comprehensive anthology of nineteenth-century commentary on Coleridge I have encountered. It retrieves valuable items that have been forgotten and remain unrecorded in standard bibliographies. It also casts a new light on a familiar landscape because the arrangement has been used to make a unique argument.

I spent pleasant hours reading and experiencing the provocation of new approaches, because many separate items are indeed new, and familiar items appear in new combinations. American Transcendentalist theologians offer a broader perspective on matters that preoccupied their Anglican counterparts. American literary scholars are juxtaposed with English reviewers, who assume an entirely different purpose in writing about their shared subject. Readers of Coleridge alternate pro and con at every level. The source of each item is in some cases evident, and where the information is not supplied, it is often suggested by some reference or other. In other cases again, it is missing altogether and, because nine-teenth- century journals for the most part were driven by strong agendas of their own, in dispute with others, I was prompted to search for clues that would locate such titles. I failed in a number of cases, as I also failed to discover the identity of even more numerous anonymous authors, but the business of searching produced other results. For example, some titles added by the compiler proved to be incorrect and those that he failed to add clarified the boundaries of his knowledge. Likewise, items one might have expected him to incorporate and that he did not, and items that at first reading appear to repeat what has been said elsewhere, help define the concerns that guided him.

While such matters gained my attention, I became curious as to who might have assembled such a collection and why. Why does the arrangement disregard chronological order? Are the odd conjunctions and apparent repetitions more than simple carelessness? What purpose did the processes of searching far and wide and then separately, of the calculated disarrangement serve? Does the book contain any clue as to why its material ends at the moment in time that it does? What kind of person had the means, opportunity and motivation to embark on such an enterprise? The resulting bound-volume shows little signs of use: there is no obvious annotation or cross-referencing of the content. It nowhere indicates that it belonged to someone who used it alongside a study of Coleridge texts. My attention thus became divided between the book and the person who put it together. The book is there—a physical object that invites one to ponder its content and argument—and it contains clues to its compiler, and how and when he worked. Why he embarked on it and the use he made of it, however, is less clear and remained a matter of speculation for much longer.

In the end it can be proved that the person who gathered and bound the materials was William Greswell (1848–1923), rector of Dodington in north-west Somerset between 1888 and 1913. The evidence of the book suggests he began collecting in the interval between graduating BA at Oxford in 1871, and ceased a few years after his ordination in 1883 as a deacon in the Church of England. The latest item in the core collection dates from September 1886, and the volume must have been arranged and bound soon after that date. (I say core collection because a few further items, the latest dating from 1893, were subsequently inserted into the binding by an unprofessional hand.) The circumstances make likely that the enterprise of collecting opinions on Coleridge, with a decided emphasis on theological matters, was connected in part with Greswell's delayed decision to take holy orders: perhaps a way of reviewing the issues involved through the judgements of others on an authority he held in particular significance. However, while this may have been Greswell's starting-point and motivation, the project ended—was literally wrapped up—in a different spirit. The sequence in which the items were finally arranged suggest he emerged from his voyage of discovery with a sense of Coleridge's restricted relevance to his spiritual needs.

A problem then arises. The Rev. William Greswell is known, if he is presently known at all, as the man on the spot when plans were set in motion in 1893 to acquire the Coleridge Cottage in Nether Stowey for the National Trust. He worked hard as secretary to the project, which concluded successfully in 1908–1909. Since the last decades of the last century, also, modern students of late Victorian imperialism have rediscovered Greswell's body of writing on colonial federation, particularly in relation to South Africa. Furthermore, following such an exhausting foray

4   J. C. C. MAYS

into a particular branch of journalism and textbook writing, which extended from 1884 to 1900 or so, he published a great deal in journal and subscription-monograph form on the early history of north-west Somerset; and there is every sign that this last subject, the geographical area between Glastonbury and the Devon border, engaged him the most dearly. In short, one must suppose the early Coleridge project led to a negative result. It was a success only in the sense that its author discovered he had less to learn from Coleridge than he had imagined. It left him with the residual feeling that Nether Stowey should remember a famous poet who had lived briefly on Lime Street, but little more.

Paradoxically, the turnaround I describe makes Greswell's anthology a document of even greater interest than I previously suggested. On one level, it portrays Coleridge as a failure of the kind that Hazlitt, Carlyle and other disillusioned hero-worshippers envisaged; as a man of wasted talents, his early promise betrayed, the subject of claims that require too much to be forgiven to justify one's trust. He needed to go no further than he did. At the same time, viewing Coleridge's influence on American transcendentalism, together with English figures like James Martineau, Walter Pater and John Rickards Mozley, Greswell picked up with a line of radical thought that was uniquely new and forward-looking; and he left it when and where he left Coleridge in the arrangement of the bound volume, pointing to the future. I mean by this last remark, not to the Coleridge of the late twentieth-century, approved by conservative Anglican revivalists, but to the line that that extends through John Seeley (Greswell's mentor on British imperialism as well as the author of *Ecce Homo* and *Natural Religion*), William Hale White and others, for whom faith is more important than dogma and is, in turn, open to change and development beyond religions. I know of no one else who brought together the trio of Martineau, Pater and Mozley as spokespersons for a Coleridge very different from Hazlitt's and Carlyle's disappointed, almost libellous campaigns. The pro-Coleridge story traditionally proceeds through the earlier trio of Julius Hare, Connop Thirlwall and F. D. Maurice, and thereafter faltered; but, if Greswell's different and more radical essayists were borne in mind, I suggest that Coleridge's standing might be very different today.

In the end, therefore, this book is not about a book but about life-issues confronting an intelligent person towards the close of the nineteenth century. The man who put it together was persuaded to work through a study of Coleridge's reputation which amounts to an idiosyncratic selection more complete than any other, composed at the time or later. In the end, Greswell drew a negative conclusion and turned onto another path. It was the obvious course to follow; no blame can be attached, and to many he will be a quiet hero. I too think the path he turned away from, as it appeared, would have landed him in a lifelong mess; but it points beyond its time to a Coleridge then barely visible, or rather visible only to a few brave and lonely voices. We now know much more about the circumstances that determined Coleridge's earlier reputation, and much more about what he intended to say since his complete writings have been published by the Bollingen Foundation. It still has not been properly realized by the general public for various reasons, although the Bollingen project has been complete for more than twenty years.

I will put the situation differently because it explains what might seem like repetition. William Greswell acted as secretary of the group that put the Coleridge Cottage into the possession of the British National Trust between 1893 and 1908–1909. He was the rector of Doddington at the time and was much less active and well-known than other members of the team like William Knight and Ernest Hartley Coleridge. His task was mainly to be the man on the spot, able to report on local feelings, which at the time were mixed. His limited aim was to rescue the cottage from the brewers and to make it a library for the use of locals who were indifferent.

By accident, I acquired this volume of nineteenth-century essays on Coleridge, made up from magazine articles and reviews, extending to some 800 pages. It was evidently compiled by someone seriously engaged with Coleridge's theological ideas, and his verse much less, and I gradually became aware that the compiler can have been no other than Greswell. This was a surprise because the more I learned about him, the less likely he appeared as somebody who involved himself deeply in theological matters.

The present book grew from such beginnings. It describes Greswell's background and childhood at Kilve, his lively education in Bath, and his progression to Oxford. He took a disappointing degree, probably due to the distraction of his developing personal interests, and afterwards moved to take up a teaching position in South Africa. He returned to write a book heavily influenced by both his African experiences and John Seeley's *Expansion of England* (1883), and continued afterwards to write on the broadening topic of British colonisation until 1899. Meanwhile, he was ordained as a deacon in 1883, set Coleridge aside sometime between 1886 and 1893, married in 1895, and then, finally, spent his last twenty years as an author of six idiosyncratic local history books, all published by subscription.

It makes an odd story: the person who compiled the largest, most provocative collection of articles on Coleridge in the nineteenth, or even twentieth, century put the lesson he learned completely behind him once the pieces were bound into a volume. And then, retrospectively teasing out the detail of what he included—and excluded—one becomes aware of an interpretation forced on him by his time, the falsehood of which has only recently been proved. An unknown book opens up the buried past and requires it to be evaluated over again.

If one reads the book in such a way, with due care, one comes to see that it falls into two parts. Part one presents a familiar Coleridge made popular by Carlyle and others: the hero promises more than he can deliver and leaves chaos and misery in his wake. Part two appears to repeat the same sad tale, but it is distinguished by three singular essays from distinctive points of view. Each of them takes a different approach and finds something of great worth. All three were written by persons outside the established church, or on what was considered at the time a loose limb of it, and they had less trouble accommodating Coleridge's ideas as these have become available in the Bollingen Coleridge. I have no idea if Greswell would have changed his mind if he had made his collection a hundred years later. Old falsehoods are often more comfortable than new truths and we may be happy to entertain them for some time yet, until the situation appears ridiculous.

The final chapter of the book will end on this note. This is followed by a selected Bibliography which I have annotated with further information.

CHAPTER 2

The Book-Object

Abstract The opening chapter discusses the book itself and what can be learned from examining its bibliographical features in more detail. For example, the date of its construction can be deduced from the two periods of its binding, professional and decidedly unprofessional. And, more obviously, how its pages are made up: for the most part out of complete articles carefully removed from their original periodicals and at other times cut out and pasted onto different kinds of paper. Each periodical is written for a different audience and comes with different presuppositions. More can be learned from the holograph-list of contents inserted into the preliminary pages, not least from the difficulties Greswell had in identifying the original place of publication of specific articles; and more again from the different papers used as backing on which articles are pasted. A number of these contain the blind-stamp address of a rectory Greswell moved into, but elected to modify one line of; another page contains a blind-stamp from a Manchester bookseller who went out of business in the 1860s; yet another registers the ownership of Bristol Public Libraries (without explanation). Then again—and most difficult of all to reproduce properly—are the signs of close reading of four particular items. They are less marginalia than pricks or pointings that an unnamed reader made as he followed the text with concentration, and they combine with numbers added to the top right-hand corner of essays a reader wanted for some reason to privilege. Three of these essays—no. **29** by James Martineau,

---

© The Author(s), under exclusive license to Springer Nature Switzerland AG 2023
J. C. C. Mays, *Coleridge in William Greswell's Workbook*,
https://doi.org/10.1007/978-3-031-38593-3_2

no. **36** by Walter Pater, and no. **45** by John Rickards Mozley—will prove to be of significance to the argument of later chapters.

Keywords What simple bibliographic details tell us • Binding • First pages • The contents-list • Blind-stamps • Signs of reading • Selected item-numbering

1 BASICS

The book entitled *Coleridge and his Writings* is exciting and important because of the material it contains and how this is arranged. At the same time, every book is put together in a way that tells something of the purpose it hopes to fulfil and this one is no exception. So, while its physical features are not what persuaded me to buy it, and I did not give them much thought until long after I became interested in its content, they in the end provided definitive answers to what emerged as key questions. Specifically, these concerned the identity of the compiler/author, the way in which he worked and the date when he thought his project was finished and was set aside.

A transitional feature of the book—that is, added after its making was complete—may be noted first. This is an undated cutting from a bookseller's catalogue—William George's Sons of Bristol, item 228—affixed to the front pastedown. It provides a summary description of the contents and names the price as three guineas (the present-day equivalent of ST£135/US$165, or more). I later suggest that the compiler was one who was born and died within fifty miles of Bristol. If this is correct, the book quite likely went on sale some time following his death, which occurred in 1923.

My comments on the book proper proceed from whole to parts, that is, begin with the binding, move to different kinds of pages and their elements and conclude with considerations of obscure pencil-marks on paper. The separate items in the book—taken from journals and newspapers—are referred to by numbers in bold: for example, Alice King's essay in *The Argosy* August 1885 as item **17**.

2   Double-Bind

The book as a book is a sturdy octavo, bound in three-quarter brown morocco. The boards are covered with matching brown watered silk, and the top cover is now faded where a smaller book lay adjacent to it undisturbed in the sun. The spine has seven raised bands embossed with gilt patterning, and the title, COLERIDGE & HIS WRITINGS, is lettered directly on the second panel in gilt caps (Illustration 2.1). Such is the book's Victorian composure that one might assume it was always thus, but this is not quite so. Leaving aside the question of when the contents of the book were collected, which must have taken place over a period of time, they evidently came together in their present form on two occasions.

The first phase of construction comprises fifty-four items that form the main body of text. The two front and rear flyleaves carry the watermarks "C. T. JEFFERIES & SONS | 1884" (Illustration 2.2): the firm that must

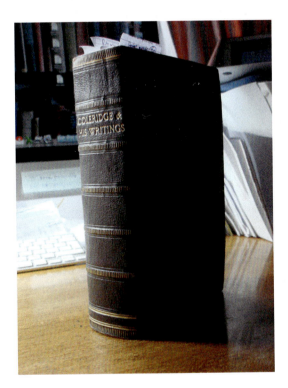

Illustration 2.1 The imposing, carefully constructed volume which is the subject of this book

Illustration 2.2 A watermark on the flyleaf reveals the date when, or soon after, the book was constructed

have done the binding. Jefferies were well-known Bristol printers of local studies, including the *Proceedings of the Bristol and Gloucestershire Archaeological Society*. Apropos the date, one of the fifty-four items—no. 17, by Charles Johnson in *Temple Bar*—dates from September 1886, which thereby settles the date when or after which the book originally came together. After the book had been bound, a two-page handwritten list of contents was pasted between the first and second of the front flyleaves.[1] One might suppose this was left free for the binder to refer to while he worked.

The second phase of construction comprises five items that follow the original fifty-four. All of them are very neatly trimmed and pasted onto notepaper of a smaller size than the pages that precede, and all five were glued together as a single block onto the first recto of the two rear flyleaves. The unprofessional insertion was a lot to swallow by a book already tightly held together and it now threatens to split the binding. Three of the inserted items date from between 1886 and 1888–1889; the fourth

---

[1] For the sake of clarity: a third flyleaf is in each case pasted onto the (rear) conjugate of the pastedown.

covers the event already described in the earlier, main sequence (no. **52**, dated 8 May 1885); and the fifth (no. **58**) covers a further event dating from June 1893. As it happens, a single brief newspaper cutting referring to the same 1893 event—as much pictorial illustration as the accompanying description in words—was pasted onto the recto of the conjugate of the first pastedown. I have labelled it as item **0** and it serves, when one has finally mastered what is going on, as an understated and almost apologetic frontispiece to the whole.

More light can be thrown on the two phases of construction by considering the details of the pages and how they are constructed.

3 Pages

The larger part of the main sequence (nos. **1–54**) comprises items that have been carefully removed from nineteenth-century journals and newspapers printed on wove paper. (The one exception is the earlier item **21**, published in the *Critical Review* in 1796, which was printed on laid paper.) The care with which the items were extracted from their original contexts—dis-bound—is such that one might even wonder if they had been received as separate offprints, or author's copies such as printers of academic journals used to provide gratis. None of them, however, is signed or addressed to a dedicatee. The variety of sources led to a collection of different page-sizes. They were aligned at the top edge by the binder, and then lightly trimmed at the right-hand side and bottom, so the slight differences of page-size are now only apparent from the two latter positions (Illustration 2.3).

When the source is not evident on the first page of printed text (as it is in e.g. nos. **2** and **34**: Illustrations 2.4 and 2.5), it is often added at the bottom right of the opening right-hand page, using either blue or black pencil. The hand that wrote the titles is the same in both cases (e.g. nos. **30** and **17** respectively: Illustrations 2.6 and 2.7), practiced but for the most part hasty. Several of the inserted titles—in black pencil, in particular—are barely comprehensible and some are incorrect. The situation as a whole suggests the task of labelling was conducted on two or more occasions, the writer being the same person albeit in different moods or under different conditions. First, hurriedly in black pencil, then again those at first passed over with more deliberation in blue. Even then success was not always achieved and three items from the Unitarian-Transcendentalist *Christian Examiner* published in Boston, Mass., are revealing: see

Illustration 2.3 The top and side of pages were once trimmed level, while the lower side remains less regular

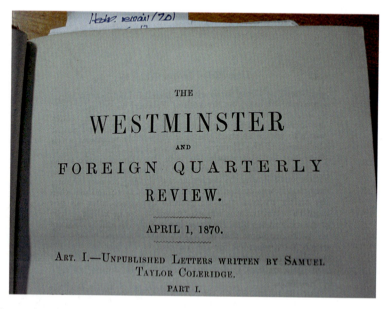

Illustration 2.4 Some extracts are already headed with full particulars

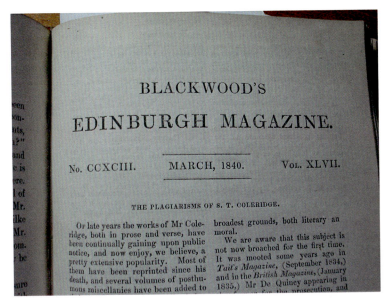

Illustration 2.5 Another example of the same

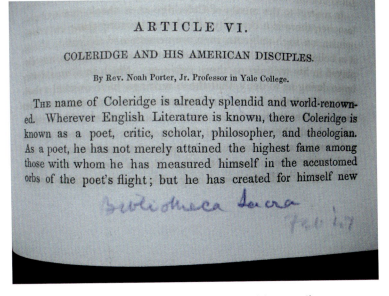

Illustration 2.6 Others have their source added in blue pencil

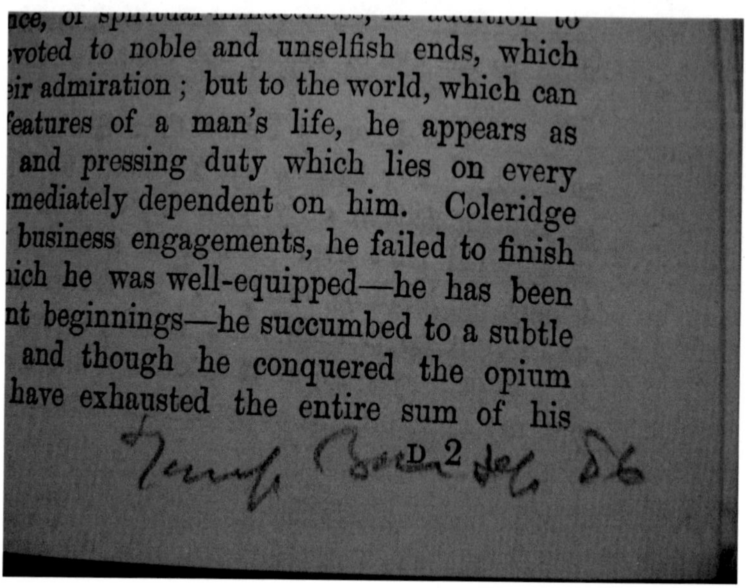
voted to noble and unselfish ends, which
ir admiration ; but to the world, which can
eatures of a man's life, he appears as
and pressing duty which lies on every
mediately dependent on him. Coleridge
business engagements, he failed to finish
ich he was well-equipped—he has been
nt beginnings—he succumbed to a subtle
and though he conquered the opium
have exhausted the entire sum of his
D 2

Illustration 2.7 Or added in black pencil. Not all the attributions are correct

Illustrations 2.8, 2.9 and 2.10. The first, item **4** is labelled correctly in black pencil with a question mark, the whole of which is then crossed through; and items **18** and **20** are labelled in blue pencil as deriving from the London *Christian Reformer*, which is incorrect. The mistake is a grave one, since the editions under review are in each case American, and the argument of item **20** is very obviously so. Again, the *Reformer* was written to address a different, more popular audience than the eminent *Examiner*. Is the repeated error due entirely to tiredness or pressure, or does it suggest that someone else collected the American items on the assembler's behalf?

The hand that wrote in blue and black pencil is problematic. It would at first appear to be different from the hand that is everywhere else involved in the making of the volume. I describe below how this appears elsewhere: (a) on a number of cut-and-pasted items, (b) on the holograph list of contents, and then again (c) on inserted memoranda that appear to be notes and reminders regarding arrangement (sequencing). The differences

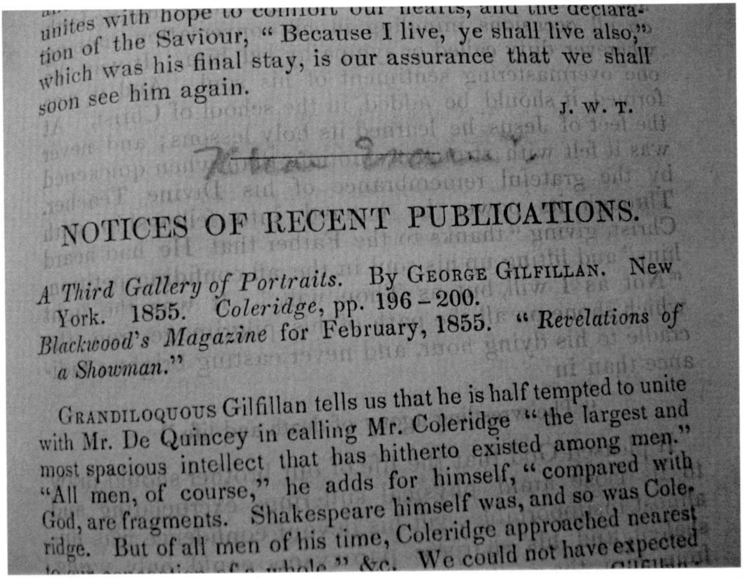

> unites with hope to comfort our hearts, and the declaration of the Saviour, "Because I live, ye shall live also," which was his final stay, is our assurance that we shall soon see him again.
>
> J. W. T.

NOTICES OF RECENT PUBLICATIONS.

A Third Gallery of Portraits. By George Gilfillan. New York. 1855. *Coleridge*, pp. 196 – 200. *Blackwood's Magazine* for February, 1855. "*Revelations of a Showman.*"

Grandiloquous Gilfillan tells us that he is half tempted to unite with Mr. De Quincey in calling Mr. Coleridge "the largest and most spacious intellect that has hitherto existed among men." "All men, of course," he adds for himself, "compared with God, are fragments. Shakespeare himself was, and so was Coleridge. But of all men of his time, Coleridge approached nearest to our imagination of a whole," &c. We could not have expected

Illustration 2.8 This ascription—in black pencil with a question mark—is the first of three references to the same magazine published in the United States. Here it is correct

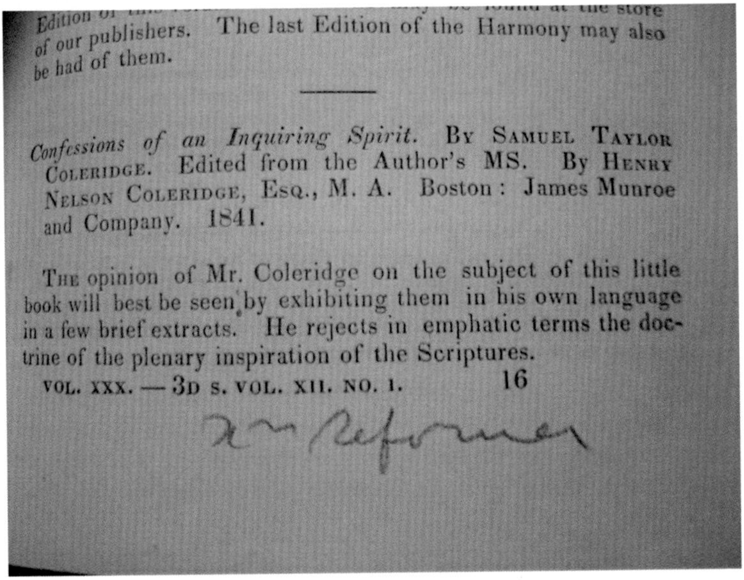

> Edition of the be found at the store of our publishers. The last Edition of the Harmony may also be had of them.
>
> _____
>
> *Confessions of an Inquiring Spirit.* By Samuel Taylor Coleridge. Edited from the Author's MS. By Henry Nelson Coleridge, Esq., M. A. Boston: James Munroe and Company. 1841.
>
> The opinion of Mr. Coleridge on the subject of this little book will best be seen by exhibiting them in his own language in a few brief extracts. He rejects in emphatic terms the doctrine of the plenary inspiration of the Scriptures.
>
> VOL. XXX. — 3D S. VOL. XII. NO. 1. 16

Illustration 2.9 But this ascription—in blue pencil—has confused the American magazine with a British periodical. (It was not the London *Christian Reformer*)

16 J. C. C. MAYS

> of what we mean ... ... see any good
> end it can accomplish, either for Christianity in general,
> or the interests of Orthodoxy in particular. Its author un-
> doubtedly saw, that, according to his doctrinal views, there
> were great deficiencies in Mr. Ware's book. He could not
> in consistency be quite satisfied with it; it was not to be
> expected. But then if it exhibits the practical excellency
> of our system, as he says, better than any other book, why
> should he labor so earnestly to destroy it? Why should he
> be so extremely unwilling that our system should exert upon
> its adherents whatever religious or moral influence it is

Illustration 2.10 A second, similar mistake in muddling an English source with an American one

between first two (a and b), both in black ink, can be explained by the cramped space available in the list of contents; the memoranda in pencil (c) are different again. Here the tentative circumstances have produced light, loosely formed characters and numerals. In short, there is such wide variation that one wonders if this might stretch to encompass the labelling of the majority of journal items; or, alternatively, if one must suppose this last was the hand of a helper. The specimens of Greswell's later handwriting (in correspondence) differ again and I see no way of answering the question.

So, to continue with pages that have not been extracted as they stand from journals and newspapers and have instead been carefully cut out, re-joined, and pasted onto separate sheets of wove paper. There are seven items of this kind in the main sequence (nos. **25, 42, 49, 51, 52, 53,** and **54: 25** and **42** as Illustrations 2.11 and 2.12), some of them with individual sheets numbered in pencil and with traces of pin-marks at top left; and, in addition, all five items of the sequence which were later inserted

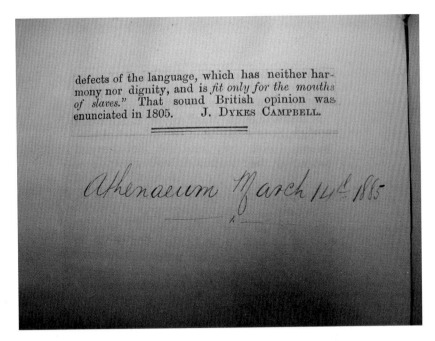

Illustration 2.11 Here, the periodical extract is cut and pasted onto wove paper

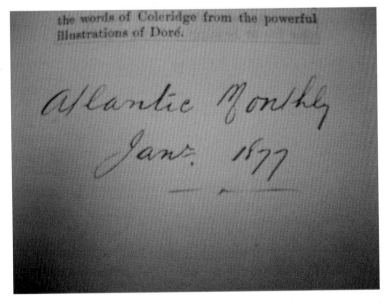

Illustration 2.12 The same again, the paper perhaps from an earlier family source

into the binding together (**55–59**). The sheets with pin-marks may derive from a single—perhaps earlier, family—source.

In the main sequence, the text of five numbers—**25**, **42**, **49**, **51** and **54**—is followed by a journal title and date in black ink, varying in its use of cursive script and capitals. Item **42** was cut from the *Atlantic Monthly*, January 1877, the same journal from which the compiler extracted a full nineteen-page article six months later in the same year (see no. **34**): the reason for the cut-and-paste job is that the "Ancient Mariner" review occupied only two of eleven pages of an omnibus review of "Recent Literature." For the remaining two items, no. **52** has the title and date inserted in blue pencil at the beginning, top right above the title, in a careful hand. And no. **53** has no inserted source-ascription. The reason in the second instance could be that the pasted-in text fills the recto page entirely and the only place for the ascription was the blank recto: it could have been omitted by oversight or by design. In the later added sequence, all five items carry a printed heading and no dates have been added by hand. Up to this point in the volume, each separate item (extract) begins on a recto page. With regard to the items added later, item **59** opens on the verso of a leaf whose recto contains the close of no. **58**, which confirms the suggestion that they were constructed and inserted as a single block.

Separate details of the pages thereby serve to confirm and extend what can be deduced from the binding, and the most important of all in its consequences has yet to be noted. The five items comprising the later-inserted section (nos. **55–59**) are pasted onto smaller-sized notepaper of a heavier stock than elsewhere. The pasted-on printed text largely covers an easily missed, blind-stamped address at the top right-hand side of each recto. This reads "The Rectory, | Dodington."—or, just possibly, "All Saints, The Rectory, | Dodington." (Illustration 2.13)—and proves the compiler was William Greswell for reasons given above in the Preface. I add that extant letters by Greswell show that he preferred to give the address as "Dodington Rectory, | Bridgwater." and had a new blind-stamp made to that effect. He must have used up the old notepaper in the thrifty fashion here described.

Greswell's thriftiness leads to another page in his volume that also contains a blind-stamp. It occurs on the bottom right-hand corner of the first page of cut-and-paste item **49** (dating from April 1885), and it records the names of Dunnill, Palmer and Co., who were Manchester booksellers who went out of business in the 1860s (Illustration 2.14). According to the *London Gazette*, 1 April 1862, the partnership was dissolved on 25 March

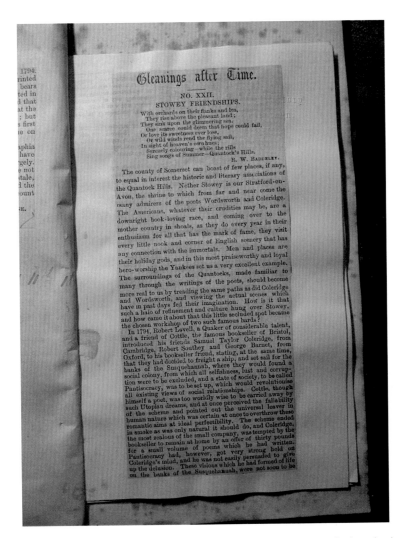

Illustration 2.13 This paste-up on Dodington Rectory paper—the imprint just visible here at top-right

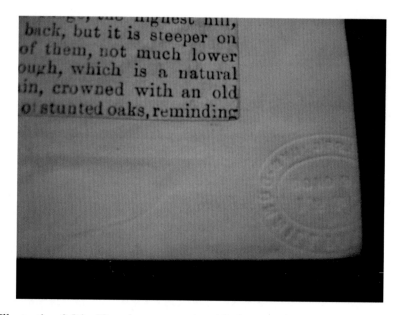

Illustration 2.14 Here the paper carries a blind stamp of a Manchester firm that went bankrupt more than twenty years before the essay pasted to it was printed

1862 and the only explanation for the paper in Greswell's book can be that he acquired or inherited it through someone with bookish interests connected with Manchester. This might have been his father, or one of his many uncles, or one of several persons associated with the present Harris Manchester College Oxford (which began as the Warrington Academy in 1757 and was located in Manchester for periods of several years during the interim). This raises the question of whether one of them assisted or even had a hand in initiating the project. And again, the Dunnill-Palmer paper provides the backing for an essay on the place in the Quantocks where Greswell grew up and I will return to this particular significance at a later stage.

Additionally, the only ink stamp in the volume—on page 5 of H. N. Coleridge's review of his own edition of *Poetical Works* 1834 (item 43/Illustration 2.15)—raises a further possibility. It forms an elongated hexagon, trimmed at the right-hand side, and now about 5.5 cm. wide and 3.0 cm. tall, with words within a frame surrounding two lines at the

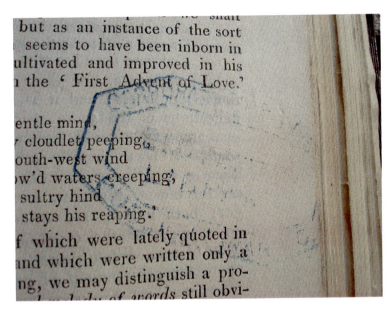

Illustration 2.15 And here the partly erased Bristol Library stamp shows the source-periodical was borrowed in the 1860s

centre. The words within the frame appear to read "CORPORAT[ION OF BRI]S[TOL]" at the top; and at the bottom, even more doubtfully, "PUBL[IC LIBR]AR[IES]." The words at the centre of the frame are obscure because there appears to have been an attempt to erase them. Such an octagonal stamp was in use in the mid-nineteenth century, according to the Bristol Libraries Stock Librarian, Howard Sykes. If the attribution is correct, this item could have been appropriated just before or at the time Greswell was an undergraduate, beginning to form his collection. There is no suggestion that any other material was gained in such an illicit way although this is of course possible.

4   Contents-List

The two list-of-contents pages are slightly smaller in size than those of the main block, and were pasted between the two front flyleaves after binding (Illustrations 2.16 and 2.17). What I have to say about them is necessarily

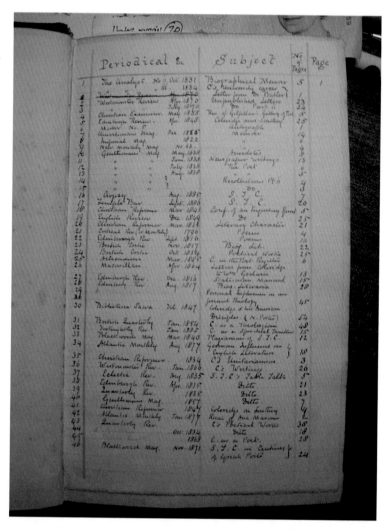

Illustration 2.16 The first of the two contents pages, with blanks that show significant uncertainty concerning the source of some items as well as other confusions

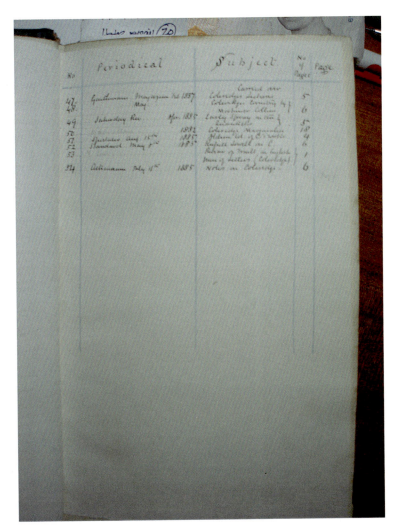

Illustration 2.17 The second contents page. Note that someone has pencilled in the number of pages in the whole

complicated and a reader may prefer to return to it later. The rectos are vertically divided by four blue pencil rules into five columns of differing widths. The first column numbers the items **1** to **54** (viz. covering the main or first-bound sequence only), although I repeat that the items are not so-numbered in the body of the volume. The second column gives the title and date of each periodical, with some revealing exceptions discussed separately below; the third column summarizes the subject in a few words (sometimes taken from an item's printed heading or running head); the fourth, the number of pages in each item; and the fifth was intended to provide the beginning-page number in the bound volume. Apropos this last, item **1** is numbered to begin on page 1, but the bound volume was not given continuous page numbering so the remainder of the fifth column remains blank. All the writing was initially in black ink. The hand is the same as that which accompanied the paste-ons, although smaller and neater to fit the available space.

However, the periodical titles of five items in column two were left blank. These titles were inserted afterwards in light (faint) pencil, in the same hand as the ink but tentatively. Thus, the periodical title supplied for item **29**—namely, the essay by James Martineau—is "?National or Prospective," the initial question mark cancelled in blue pencil. Both of the named periodicals were Unitarian in flavour and Martineau contributed to both of them; indeed, was instrumental in the setting up of the *National*. The *Prospective Review* (1845–1854) had a narrow circulation and was conservative in its views. The *National Review*, which succeeded it (1855–1864), published one of the first reviews of Darwin's *Origin of Species*, and was edited by Richard Bagehot and Richard Holt Hutton under Martineau's direct, overall direction.

Next, the contents-page gives only the date of item **44**—the review of *Poetical Works* 1834 by John Wilson—in ink, which *could* have been derived from the running-heads. The space for the title is left blank, "?Gentleman's" was pencilled in, and the question mark has a cancellation mark beside it in blue pencil. The guess is probably based upon the text being printed in double columns, like the several items by Daniel Stuart (nos. **10–13**). It actually comes from *Blackwood's*, which was also printed in double columns (see nos. **33, 46** and **50**).

Third, item **45**—Mozley on Coleridge as poet—gives the correct date in ink, but again leaves the space for the title blank. The date *could* have been derived from the volume- and issue-number at the foot of several pages. "British Quart." has been pencilled in here for the title in the contents list, but this is a mistake. The correct source is the *Quarterly Review* (as in items **39** and **43**). For the nonconformist *British Quarterly Review*, see item **31** on Coleridge as theologian, where the journal was correctly identified.

Fourth, item **50**: Helen Zimmern on marginalia. The contents-page gives the correct date in ink, deriving it from the running heads, and leaves the space for the title blank. "Macmillan" has been pencilled in, but the correct title is *Blackwood's*. The same lack of familiarity resulted in a different guess for item **44** (see above).

Fifth, item **53**: the anonymous review of Traill's monograph on a joined-up paste-in. The contents-page leaves the space for the title and date blank; and this has been filled in, in pencil, with "?Cont." I did not trace the source myself.

The final entry (no. **54**) on the original list of contents is followed, in the extreme right-hand column, by a pencil insertion of the numeral 797—which I take as a count of the total number of pages of text.

The confusion of items from *Blackwood's* (nos.**44** and **50**) is odd. The ignorance concerning the origins of the pieces by Martineau and Mozley (nos. **29** and **45**) is certainly so, given their evidently important role in the composition of the sequence. It adds weight to the possibility that Greswell could have been substantially reliant on another person for the supply of the items he eventually bound.

5   Marks on Pages

I remarked earlier that Greswell's book shows very few signs of having been read, in part or in whole. There are no turned-down corners, marginal cross-references, obvious comments or corrections, and no underlining. The only signs are restricted to four items: first, items **29** and **53**, the essay by Martineau and the review of Traill; and second, the essays by Pater and Mozley, items **36** and **45**. These are all black pencil markings of the same distinctive kind and so presumably made by the same person. They escaped my attention for a long time, until I began to read with a magnifying glass, being made up of dots and dashes the length of a hyphen (sometimes curved), the dots sometimes in the margins and both sorts otherwise scattered between lines of the text (where they often might apply to the passage above or below). The first pair differs from the second in being made up of marks that are much more specific: I mean, geared to particular words and phrases within the lines of print.

The long Martineau essay contains evidence of the most intense scrutiny. Marks appear on at least twelve of the twenty-odd pages devoted to

Newman, five of the ten pages devoted to Coleridge, and four of the ten devoted to Carlyle. At the same time, many of these pages contain more than one such mark, and they are particularly plentiful on the Coleridge pages. Page 474 of Martineau contains five such markings (partial Illustration 2.18) that are representative: evidence of someone reading carefully, marking out the stages of a skilful exposition. The markings on the review of Traill (which fills just a single cut-and-paste recto) are fainter and their significance is more ambiguous (Illustration 2.19). The review comes down on the side of Coleridge's metaphysics and theology, against Traill, but where the reader stood with pencil in hand is a moot question. Do the marks twenty-four, twenty-three, nineteen and sixteen lines from the end of the page sum up an agreement with Traill's dismissal of Coleridge's thinking or with the unidentified reviewer's dismissal of Traill?

The markings on the essays by Pater and Mozley are predominantly of a different kind. They appear on seven pages up to and including page 117 of the first, and on nine pages up to and including page 101 of the second. All but one of the marks on the Pater pages are in the top, bottom or side

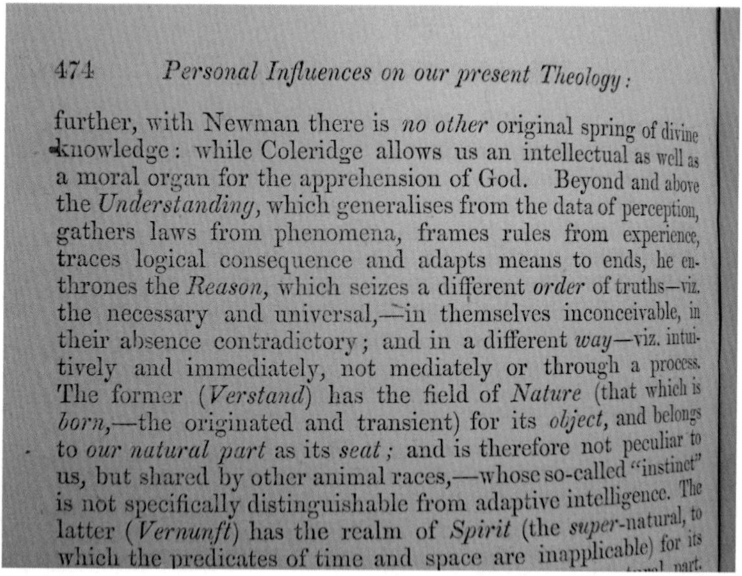

474 *Personal Influences on our present Theology:*

further, with Newman there is *no other* original spring of divine knowledge: while Coleridge allows us an intellectual as well as a moral organ for the apprehension of God. Beyond and above the *Understanding*, which generalises from the data of perception, gathers laws from phenomena, frames rules from experience, traces logical consequence and adapts means to ends, he enthrones the *Reason*, which seizes a different *order* of truths—viz. the necessary and universal,—in themselves inconceivable, in their absence contradictory; and in a different *way*—viz. intuitively and immediately, not mediately or through a process. The former (*Verstand*) has the field of *Nature* (that which is *born*,—the originated and transient) for its *object*, and belongs to *our natural part* as its *seat*; and is therefore not peculiar to us, but shared by other animal races,—whose so-called "instinct" is not specifically distinguishable from adaptive intelligence. The latter (*Vernunft*) has the realm of *Spirit* (the *super*-natural, to which the predicates of time and space are inapplicable) for its

Illustration 2.18 The top portion of a page of James Martineau's essay, with five-minute pencilled indications of how carefully it was studied

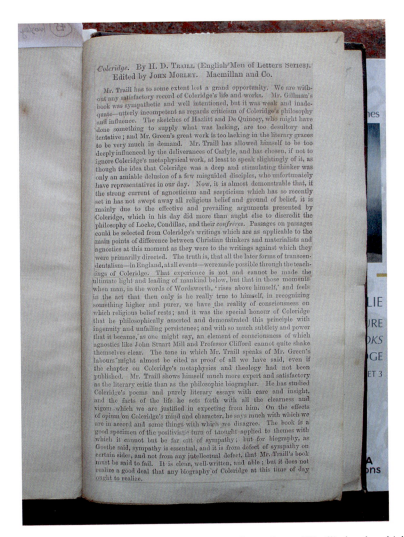

Illustration 2.19 Four similar markings on the review of Traill's book, which leave one wondering where the person who made them stands

margins of the text, and thereby make more general references to a body of text, as distant from words and phrases (as in the Martineau and Traill essays). The same for the Mozley essay: only three of the nine marks are specific (within the printed lines of text). I should also add that all the markings of the second kind are fainter than the first: indeed, that a good number are very questionable. They might not have been made with much sense of purpose, or accidentally.

In addition to such markings—or should they be called pricks or pointings that survive to register how four particular items were read—a number of black pencil numerals were inserted through the volume. They are quite differently connected with the placement (sequence) of items and so might be taken for granted as a routine matter, but they throw light on the decisions made.

Thus, the first page (recto) of item **1** contains—besides the name of the journal and date at the bottom right of the page—the book-title, "Coleridge & his Writings," written in black pencil over the printed running-head, and "p. 7" below it in the top right-hand margin (Illustration 2.20). It is clearly an instruction to the binder to begin here: the conjugate

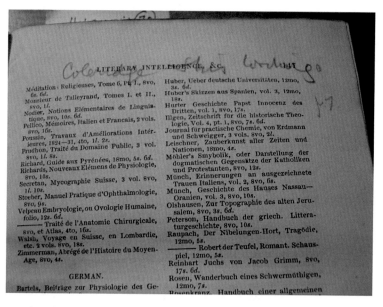

Illustration 2.20   The author's instruction to the binder: to begin the collection at this point, leaving the previous six pages to be inserted later

of the front pastedown and the following two flyleaves making six "pages" (that is, not counting the two contents-list pages pasted in later). This is indeed a simple instruction—book mechanics—but the way it opens into the book as a whole was very exactly calculated. The degree to which one can rely on a memoir written by an old acquaintance in a provincial journal, in all simplicity and good faith, is severely questioned when one comes to understand the subtext of the items that follow, as will become apparent.

The first page of item **21** has the journal title in firm black pencil written over the title, at mid-page, and a neat "22" written in faint black pencil at the top right-hand corner. The first page of item **24** has the journal title in blue pencil written at the bottom of the page, and a black-pencil numeral "25" neatly inserted in the top right- hand corner (Illustration 2.21). One can suppose the enumerator included the addendum to item one (the October issue of *The Analyst*) separately when he made his count, and absorbed the addendum into the first item when he constructed the handwritten list of contents. He was clearly managing his sequence with care. However, the matter of placement raises the question of why item **24** is separated from the two other reviews of Coleridge's 1834 *Poetical Works* (items **43** and **44**)—a more suitable position among a succession of verse volumes. I will return to the question of why this review by Joseph Sortain was so privileged on a later page.

As noted already apropos the handwritten list of contents, there was some uncertainty about the source of item **29**. The tentative guesses suggest a Unitarian journal, probably because the author was known to be James Martineau. No ascription appears on the first page, only two numerals: a neat black-pencil numeral "31" (in the style of the "22" and "25" first written on items **21** and **24**) in the top right-hand corner, and a larger, more hastily written "26" below to the left (Illustration 2.22). I suggest that "31" was written at the earliest stage of arrangement, brought forward to "26," and found its present place after further re-arrangement of the previous items. The intention appears to have been—or became—that it should occupy the central position in the physical book. It is not the longest essay—the one following (**30**), by Noah Porter, enjoys that distinction—but it is the one the compiler apparently spent the most time over, puzzling through its meaning. Indeed, as I hope I to show, it embodies a turning point in several respects: a point after which the arrangement repeats itself differently, to make a different point. What appeared relatively straightforward becomes richer, if more elusive.

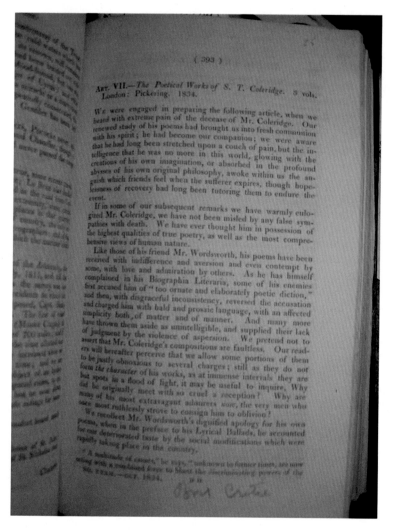

Illustration 2.21 The inserted pencil number 24 keeps this essay by Joseph Sortain here, in this place, separate from the two other reviews of Coleridge's *Poetical Works* (1834)

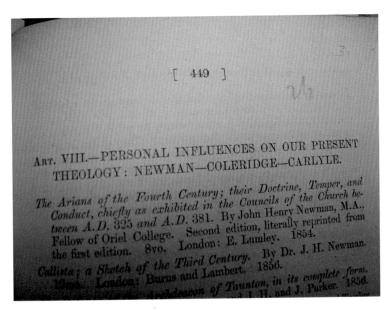

Illustration 2.22 James Martineau's essay, with corrected numerals that reveal the care (and uncertainty) with which it was placed in the central position

The last item concerned is Mozley on Coleridge as poet (no. **45**). I noted above that the contents list revealed uncertainty over the source's title. Two letters that look like "Fr" were written first in the bottom margin of the opening page (a recto) and then overwritten by a very hastily scrawled "Qy Jly/68"—all in black pencil (Illustration 2.23). "Fr" perhaps stood for a guess at the *Fortnightly Review*, but the correct ascription to the *Quarterly Review* July 1868 must have been pencilled in after the contents list was made and revisited (see above on the list). This said, the hastily written character in black pencil that appears in the top right-hand corner of the opening recto might read as the numeral 8 (or 5?) or the character d (Illustration 2.24). It might simply be a sign to draw attention to a problematic entry. I can only say that it is difficult to see how it would fit among the early entries of the sequence and that it is, at the same time, a contribution of some consequence. Its author was a nephew of the brothers John Henry Newman and Francis Henry Newman, whose opposite views he canvassed, and a prominent member of advanced Cambridge circles (the Grote Club, etc.) in which Greswell took an interest. The

;hest object of its solicitude, ~~in India,~~ inasmuch
nt of the country and the well-being of its ~~very raison~~
viding a rapid and cheap mode of con-
 the country from one province to another,
 serves to develop the agricultural resources
ltiply articles of cultivation, and to give a
rsuits of industry. As far as its influence
extends,

Illustration 2.23 The details of Mozley's essay also corrected, showing the care with which its proper source was pursued

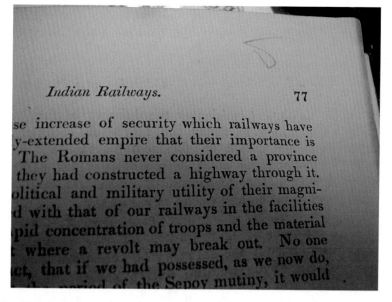

Indian Railways.   77

se increase of security which railways have
y-extended empire that their importance is
 The Romans never considered a province
they had constructed a highway through it.
olitical and military utility of their magni-
d with that of our railways in the facilities
pid concentration of troops and the material
 where a revolt may break out. No one
ct, that if we had possessed, as we now do,
   of the Sepoy mutiny, it would

Illustration 2.24 The head of the page that contains Mozley's essay, with the illegible number or letter that again displays concern and uncertainty as to where the essay should be placed

essay, perhaps unconvincing in itself, is representative of an important larger argument, and the pressure Greswell clearly felt to track down his source when his volume was otherwise complete is not insignificant.

All these uncertainties will be shown to be important in later chapters, but it is meanwhile necessary to catch up with different first impressions of the book, that is, with my own first impressions of its contents.

CHAPTER 3

The Way In

Abstract The main features of Greswell's collection are given a preliminary survey, which extends widely and needs explanation. The rich admixture of American contributions is notable because it introduces a more detached note into the consideration of Coleridge's theology which the home-grown British contributions lack. Greswell is not always sure where these essays derive from, but he plays them very effectively against one another from the very beginning. Again, because the material was first printed in periodicals—he took care to provide the *titles* more than the authors—they possess the cutting directness that periodical-writing requires. Greswell's choice necessarily lacks some element of the reflexive, more nuanced quality that book-publication can afford but it is, at the same time, very much to the moment. Overall, one might take it this charged offsetting is the way the primary argument primarily develops, through to Martineau's essay (no. **29**), which thereafter goes back to beginnings in order to go forward. Then the larger argument repeats itself over again and drifts—and has nowhere to go but too far or not far enough—and the installation of the bust in Westminster Abbey is a fair if somewhat dismissive conclusion. The story goes round in circles, which get smaller every time. Perhaps the Coleridge Cottage has to be rescued in Greswell's mind from the publicans; perhaps in Greswell's mind it could have become a library, but not a lot more.

© The Author(s), under exclusive license to Springer Nature
Switzerland AG 2023
J. C. C. Mays, *Coleridge in William Greswell's Workbook*,
https://doi.org/10.1007/978-3-031-38593-3_3

36   J. C. C. MAYS

Keywords Matter • The subject of nineteenth-century English and American periodicals • Listing titles and not authors • How this twists the argument • A vague argument emerges and is repeated • To what end?

1   TAKEN FOR GRANTED

My first encounter with Greswell's book left me surprised, excited and bewildered because it contains so much that is new in no obvious arrangement. Before listing the contents, I want to describe some contingent factors to be born in mind: they underlie the choices he made, his omissions and his apparent duplications. Put another way, Greswell made his book for his own use. It was unnecessary for him to explain his starting-point and working assumptions, but they can be deduced from the way he worked. They are ordinary enough for a man of his sort, given the place and time in which he lived, but they are specific to that time and certainly different from the circumstances of today.

What must be taken for granted is Greswell's basic conventionality. He came from a family of orthodox Anglican clergymen and followed in their footsteps: there is only the slightest hint that he ever thought to do otherwise and it caused him to delay, not alter, direction. At the same time, traditional though his values were, he was one of a generation that looked back on a century of enormous change. The face of England had altered in every respect—demographically, culturally, politically—and the alterations were felt particularly in the area of religious belief. Rapid advances in science, and even more in the application of empirical ways of thinking at large, appeared to undermine long-unchallenged truths. Religion, with its privileged place in the discussion of first and last things, saw seismic changes of attitude. The established Church of England had been rocked in turn by an Evangelical Revival, Tractarianism, Newman and the flight to Rome, Utilitarianism and a new understanding of the status of Biblical texts that only some dissenting congregations were able to take in their stride. These events are part of history, but they are not in Greswell's book; or, more accurately, they are there only at the fringes. Any representative selection of Coleridge's place in nineteenth-century thought would nowadays have to include John Stuart Mill's 1840 essay in the *Westminster Review*—perhaps also the companion essay on Bentham from two years before—but Greswell takes them for granted. As far as the Philosophic

Radical line on Coleridge is included, it is subtly represented by later contributions from the *Westminster* (items **2, 3** and **36**) that bear more concisely (if obliquely) on questionable aspects of Coleridge's influence.

Put another way, Greswell's selection is drawn from texts that extend across more than ninety years: from 1796 to 1886, extending to 1893, but it was made towards the end of that period. One might set it alongside John Tulloch's *Movements of Religious Thought in Britain during the Nineteenth Century* published in 1885, which maps a clear narrative that begins with Coleridge and ends with Benjamin Jowett and James Martineau. Greswell and Tulloch selectively cover the same territory with different intent. It is not just that Greswell is concerned to include all aspects of Coleridge's claim to fame—in particular, in verse as well as prose, in areas like literary criticism as well as theology—and Tulloch is concerned solely with theology. Greswell's interest lies in the viability and present application of Coleridge's theology but selectively, and to such an extent, that one only begins to discern his special interest properly if one bears Tulloch's more representative survey in mind. In addition, one needs to take note of events—disturbances—that bear little direct connection to Coleridge at all: the controversy over baptismal regeneration caused by the Gorham Case (1847–1850), the series of controversies aroused by Bishop Colenso's historical researches (from 1855 onwards), the furore following the publication of *Essays and Reviews* (1860), and John Seeley's anonymous *Ecce Homo* (1866). A shift was taking place: more churches were being built while old ties were loosening; the Unitarians, of all denominations one might think inappropriately, revived a version of Gothic architecture that became *de rigueur* across a wide spectrum, High Church and Low Church alike. Greswell's project, put together over a decade or more leading up to 1886, took a lot of history silently for granted and used a long view to clarify one issue as it bore at the time that was.

What Greswell took for granted was nicely illustrated by Rosemary Ashton in an essay entitled "Doubting Clerics: From James Anthony Froude to *Robert Elsmere* via George Eliot." Froude's autobiographical novel, *The Nemesis of Faith* (1849), is a crude but explicit statement of religious doubt and disillusionment. It caused an uproar at Oxford when it was published over its author's name, and it was publicly burned before Froude resigned his college fellowship. *Robert Elsmere* (1888) is, in essence, a revision of the same plot. It was written by Mrs. Humphry Ward (a niece of Matthew Arnold who married a Brasenose tutor) in reaction to

38   J. C. C. MAYS

the strongly orthodox Bampton Lecture of 1881 given by John Wordsworth, another fellow of Brasenose and great-nephew of the poet. Her narrative of a protagonist who withdraws from his ordinary priestly functions to become, in effect, a social worker serving the poor and disadvantaged and which in turn caused considerable controversy. The two novels encapsulate a contrast between two eras: in the earlier, the protagonist is crushed by a rigid orthodoxy, and in the later one, another protagonist, in a similarly painful situation, is able to find a productive way forward. Froude's novel retained its totemic status through the century although it did not sell well: Mrs. Ward's was the bestseller of its day in Britain and North America, and this was not only because it is better written. A shift in the nature of religion took place in the English mind in the period following the mid-century and, for the majority, matters of dogma came to count for less than matters of faith. This then was the peculiar starting-position of Greswell's project: as a prospective ordinand, he put a book together with the practical purpose of assessing what Coleridge had to offer.

2   PERIODICALS, NOT BOOKS

Greswell pursued his project through reviews and review-essays of Coleridge material: not through what are now called primary texts. And he extracted this secondary material from periodicals and newspapers, not from book-length studies.

One might think this a matter of convenience or a self-imposed rule of proceeding, but it excluded, for example, Fenton's Hort's essay in *Cambridge Essays* (1856), which would otherwise have deserved representation at least in part. Another item I myself should have liked to have seen included, because it is too often passed over, is Derwent Coleridge's extended "Introductory Essay" to the 1870 edition of his father's poems. It was the final edition of many such published by Moxon, in which the last surviving child speaks his mind in a way he had been reluctant to do before. In the event, space is found for a wide-ranging, seventy-six page essay from the New York *Bibliotheca Sacra* (no. **30**) that repeats much already said elsewhere.

However, I think a case can be made for Greswell's concentration on periodicals as a deliberate part of his design: that is, his taking for granted a large area of source material in order to concentrate on the selection he is trying to make. Not only are texts by Coleridge taken for granted but also the larger background of ideas connected with widely known book-authors. Hazlitt's essay on Coleridge in *The Spirit of the Age* (1825) is a good example. It opens "The present is an age of talkers; and the reason is, that the world is growing old," and it thereby laid down a challenge for reviewers of the *Table Talk* (here items **37–40**) to accept or pick up in a different way. Equally and more famously, the marvellous invocation that opens Chap. 8 of Carlyle's *Life of John Sterling* (1851)—of Coleridge as an emblem of disappointed hopes, his voice contracted to "a plaintive snuffle"—must have been present, at one level or another, in the mind of every subsequent nineteenth-century reader of Coleridge. Indeed, the entire opening paragraph could have been chosen to stand as the epigraph of Greswell's book: was its subject true, false, fair or a total misrepresentation?

The most important feature of the kind of writing Greswell drew upon comes from its being predominantly made up of reviews: not for the most part long-considered commentary on Coleridge texts, but immediate responses. And while different publishers make and sell recognizably different kinds of books, the publishers of periodicals and newspapers work under the specific necessity of finding groups of readers who will loyally subscribe. The periodicals Greswell drew upon all advertise blatant principles and prejudices, as do those he chose not to include, and the life of his book is their relationship to one another as this is reflected in Coleridge. What Coleridge's readers found to approve and disapprove in the multi-faceted mirror is especially clear, and some statistics and reflections thereon will be useful here.

The sixty items—comprising essays and reviews, plus a few brief notes—are drawn from thirty-one different periodicals. Twenty-nine of the periodicals are identifiable and the remaining two date from the close of the main series (that is, in 1885 and in 1885–1886). Nineteen periodicals are drawn upon once, five are drawn upon twice, two are drawn upon thrice and three periodicals are drawn upon more than four times. The dates of appearance are spread fairly evenly, with two bulges: in the 1830s (following Coleridge's death), and again in the 1870s and 1880s (up to the time the process of collecting was abandoned). One might reckon that the items published before Coleridge's death and soon after contain the material that is now most familiar (at least to literary students familiar with the "Critical Companion" series and the like); here intermingled, it must be said, with disconcerting oddities. Alongside them, items drawn from the period when the collection was probably in progress contain the bulk of

40   J. C. C. MAYS

material that was only drawn upon once. In retrospect, it is natural for the search for material that settled into place decades beforehand to be more deliberate than forty years later, after the search got underway, when chance occasions provided wider opportunities. At the same time, several particularly lengthy essays that might be considered of importance date from the 1850s and 1860s, and perhaps they were searched out—as they appear to have been placed (see Chap. 2 above: Sect. 5)—with particular care.

I also passed over an unusual aspect of the naming of items in Chap. 2, where the primary interest was their orthography. They are tagged with the titles of the *periodicals* they come from, and only once (the longest article in the contents list) with the name of their author. The redoubled attempt at inscribing the titles, in black and then blue pencil, was of obvious importance to Greswell, and it is of similar importance to anyone who would follow his intent. Thus, the inclusion of articles/reviews from four different American sources is notable; and one such—the *Christian Examiner*—provides three such items across a span of twenty years. While the theological background of the four periodicals is different, the shared longer view they provide is unlike that of most English journals. One might say that in its detachment it feels closest to the person who collected and arranged them.

Then the competing politics of the great earlier nineteenth-century Scottish and English reviews—*Blackwood's*, the *Edinburgh* and the *Quarterly*—had become part of history by the time the anthology was assembled. And one may suspect that they were in part included here for that reason, for the record, and that the *Gentleman's Magazine* was used in a similar manner: to get something said that was no longer a bone of contention. Greswell's selection takes special note of how the individual items are used. It would appear that the chronologically earlier ones register moments in a familiar history, and could be said to remain relatively inert ("for the record"), while those from later sources more actively engage with a more pressing sense of legacy ("and now?"). This feature causes earlier questions to mutate into a different category: what is Coleridge's authority in an altered context, which is becoming more liberal in different ways?

From another perspective, one needs to bear in mind that the *Westminster Review* under John Chapman's editorship published strong pieces by George Eliot, Francis Newman, Herbert Spencer and the like; that *Macmillan's Magazine* was founded by an admirer of F. D. Maurice, whose early contributions established its more centrist character; and that the *Fortnightly Review* was different again in what may be described as, for the most part, its more secular liberalism. Various different streams of religious persuasion are evident, and while one side is allowed more room to develop its views—in the nonconformist *British Quarterly* and the Unitarian *Christian Reformer* and *National Review*—the high church *British Critic* and *English Review* are also given strong billing. So it is also in literary matters. There are magazines that exist to puff and excoriate (for example, the *New Monthly*) alongside others founded consciously to raise the standard of literary reviewing (the *Eclectic Review* and *Temple Bar*). It is frequently not easy to interpret how tagging each item with the known reputation of the journal in which it appeared is intended to be more than purely descriptive: for instance, the *Westminster Review* was founded by Jeremy Bentham as the official organ of the Philosophic Radicals in 1824. No wonder that it published Pater's essay in 1866 (item **36**), but the fact that it published what at first sight looks like a scholarly contribution on a dimly-known period in Coleridge's biography in 1870 (items **2** and **3**) makes one think again. The intention here was not so innocent, as Chap. 6 will show.

I must also add before going further that the impression given that the compilation covers the full range of Coleridge's interests and publication is belied by the omission of any separate commentary on the *Constitution of the Church and State* (1829, 2nd ed. 1830). The relationship discussed under that title was of great concern to Coleridge, as his opposition to Catholic Emancipation showed, and as it was to all those who did not subscribe to the Thirty-Nine Articles. Subscription was required by the Church of England to matriculate at Oxford (up to 1854), to proceed to a degree at Cambridge (1856), and for ordination. The relation between church and state can only have been unproblematic for Greswell because his mind was settled in an Anglican mould. His project was to test and affirm broadly orthodox beliefs and practice against reactions to Coleridge under different headings, not to do anything like replace them.

3   Rough Guide

The overall arrangement may be said to override the date when items were published in order to work on a principle that is thematic. It opens with what appears to be a conventional memoir (and supplement), followed by more recently disclosed details from Coleridge's middle life (from the time he lived in Calne, whence he later went to Highgate) and a succession of further personal recollections and general assessments from contrasting points of view. Thus, a generous backward view of his theological ideas in an American (Episcopal) journal (item **7**) is immediately followed by a couple of undistinguished pieces from English magazines, which contribute nothing new except errors. Four fact-filled contributions to the *Gentleman's Magazine* by Daniel Stuart change the tone (nos. **10–13**), and they are again counterpointed by much later-published and less important reflections on Coleridge by the Cowden Clarks (nos. **14–15**).

At this point, items **16** and **17** appear to have been deliberately inserted to punctuate the irregular progression. They celebrate Coleridge first as a local and then as a major poet, first for a popular audience and then as an object of academic study. Both in their different ways engage with their intended audience, but they leave one wondering what to think. Does it just depend on whom you are talking to? At all events, the next two essays again shift gear as they review successive editions of *Confessions of an Inquiring Spirit*: the first (American) accepts Coleridge's argument whole, with a wry protest against his style before it leaves off, and the second (English) disagrees with its argument virulently. A third essay (item **20**) is again from an American source and, as it happens, strikes a balance that proved to be particularly influential in Unitarian and Transcendentalist circles. It certainly marks the close of an interval in which the mixed biographical items ended and a series of other issues were raised.

Item **21** inaugurates this fresh direction, returning as it does to a review of Coleridge's 1796 *Poems*. A sequence of early literary reviews follows that take up with *The Statesman's Manual* and *Biographia Literaria,* and accommodate Coleridge's letters to Godwin. This last (no. **26**) is not entirely anomalous. Godwin was the son of a dissenting Sandemanian minister and was educated at the radical new Hoxton Academy under Andrew Kippis. Subsequently a rationalist atheist, he became a vague deist under Coleridge's influence. He stands here alongside the anonymity of several Unitarian authors (e.g. no. **21**) and the nonconformity of Joseph Sortain (no. **24**)—perhaps a reminder of his capacity for friendship or of his unsound judgement.

Indeed, the sequence concludes in item **29** with James Martineau's lengthy and far- ranging discussion of Coleridge, which as I observed seems to have been placed here deliberately at the heart of the volume. It does indeed introduce a decided shift of tone. Item **30**—on "Coleridge and his American Disciples" by a Congregational minister—is, as noted before, the longest essay in the volume. Others that follow on mainly theological subjects maintain the same level of serious enquiry until, after item **35**, which again reminds us directly of Coleridge's withdrawal from the Shrewsbury Unitarian meeting. Pater's essay on Coleridge as theologian is incorporated as item **36**.

At this late point, the focus changes yet again: it goes back in order to move forward in a different way. Four items (**37–40**) cover *Table Talk* and the issue of whether Coleridge, the talker, took the easy option and failed to commit himself to the real job of writing. Item **41**, which is actually a review of a selection from Coleridge's marginalia on Southey's *Life of Wesley*, contributes to the same subtext in a way which does not question Coleridge's genius, but instead his ability to formulate an extended, coherent argument. (Item **50** on his hitherto unpublished marginalia returns to the same issue.) Meanwhile, item **42**—a cutting from the *Atlantic Monthly* on Doré's illustrated "Ancient Mariner"—picks up again with reviews of Coleridge's poetry that left off with item **25**. This includes the largely dull (items **43, 44**), which in time became the largely conventional (no. **46**), but at its heart is Mozley's attempt to make a case for Coleridge's later poetry and argue that he was, all told, a greater poet than Wordsworth (no. **45**). Whatever its merits and failings, one must say that this last is persistently argued and that, in my view, is Greswell's point.

From here to the close, the sense of an impossible larger argument and the nature of the arrangement are left to drift. Coleridge is defended as a lecturer (item **47**), on the same restricted grounds as his *Table Talk*; there are essays that cite local allusions in his poems (nos. **48–49**); two reviews of Ashe's new edition note that it does not add much of worth (nos. **51, 54**); a review of Traill's new "Man of Letters" study regrets the lack of interest in ideas (no. **53**). On a similarly loose rein, a newspaper report of Lowell's speech on the newly installed bust of Coleridge in Westminster Abbey is also included (no. **52**); and the same event again in the inserted addition to the main series (no **59**), along with a tripartite series on literary figures associated with Stowey (nos. **55–57**), and a much later newspaper report on plans to save the Cottage (no. **58** and see also no. **0**).

So the configuration comes to a meandering close. It has a loose shape—biographical information succeeded by reviews of verse and prose that have different kinds of Unitarian connection; Martineau's essay at the physical middle of the book, leading to a second half that focuses more sharply on Coleridge's thinking and includes two more unexpected major pieces—by Pater and by Mozley—before the ensemble breaks up among publications and events of the moment. There are sharp turns between subject-matter and the levels of discussion; a continuous run of reviews of books related to the same topic can be marked off by a couple of reviews on an entirely different subject; things one expects to find make unexpected ones more important. In the case of the American contributions, this last feature makes them appear for the most part more authoritative: in the case of the English, it tends to make them more provocative. All told, the arrangement is intuitive but effective, and I will return to enlarge upon its deeper agenda in Chap. 8. Enough has meanwhile been said to prepare for what to expect, and more will be added when the individual Contents have been listed.

CHAPTER 4

The Contents as They Stand

Abstract The contents of Greswell's book are described in the order in which they appear (e.g. with their added number in bold), with only his errors of title-transcription corrected in a note. They are accompanied by brief notes on the author and where relevant, the occasion of the essay. Greswell's choice of reviews tiptoed between difficult choices: every one arrived with a set of unstated fierce assumptions; and he reached their final arrangement after he had given the matter considerable thought. The result contains the essence of his judgement, crossed with feelings he hardly wanted to entertain yet somehow did. How else to summarise what is so simple to say?

The book contains sixty entries; they have been carefully removed from thirty-one journals and newspapers published in Great Britain and the USA. A good number of the printed items contain a statement of their origin at or near their beginning; others have it inserted, often in abbreviated form, somewhere on the first or facing page. Others, which are pasted onto different-sized pieces of paper, have their sources inserted in pen or pencil, and some of these attributions (English and American) were wrong; and this may indicate they came from another helper. Other marks—in pencil and in ink—that occur in these pages are not noted here.

Keywords A complete listing of the contents • Items listed in detail • Significant wrong attributions • Different physical means of extracting

© The Author(s), under exclusive license to Springer Nature Switzerland AG 2023
J. C. C. Mays, *Coleridge in William Greswell's Workbook*, https://doi.org/10.1007/978-3-031-38593-3_4

45

46 J. C. C. MAYS

them from their sources • Different means of describing their origins •
An argument firms up

The present chapter is basic to my interpretation of Greswell's book. From
it, at least in theory, the whole of his enterprise could be re-constructed if
my unique copy went up in smoke. I have not reproduced the listing of
items exactly as they appear (often incorrectly) but, at the same time, I
have not rearranged them in chronological order in order to match
present-day expectations. My understanding is that the original arrangement is calculated deliberately to make an argument on behalf of an understanding of Coleridge's place in history and, at best, it contains an amount
of truth that has passed others by.

Items **1–54** constitute the volume as professionally bound between
1886 and 1889, as described in Chap. 1. Items **0** and **55–60** were inserted
sometime soon after mid-1893. I have separated them from the core
entries below by rows of asterisks. I have also corrected mistakes and supplied omissions wherever I could in my listing. The comments that follow
in each entry, in smaller blue print, supply additional information that a
present-day reader may find useful. Some of them repeat and others
enlarge upon information already given in the main text. I have used
abbreviations for Coleridge texts as they appear in the Bollingen Collected
Coleridge: *CL* for *Collected Letters* ed. Griggs, *CN* for *Notebooks* ed.
Coburn, *SW&F* for *Shorter Works and Fragments*, *CM* for *Marginalia*,
STC for Coleridge himself, etc.

---

0. Anon. "Coleridge's Cottage at Nether Stowey." *The Daily Graphic.*
With an illustration by D. Burke.

A downbeat estimation of the building, the village and the Coleridge connection. The day of publication was a Monday, and it is noted as "From a
Correspondent." Published after the tablet was affixed *above* the door of the
building on 9 June 1893 (see item **58** below) and was still a recent event.
The newspaper cutting (with narrow columns) was pasted onto the front
free endpaper, which carries the watermark 1884.

One supposes this item was prefixed to the collection after it had been
bound, at about the time the additional items had been inserted at the close.

*   *   *

4 THE CONTENTS AS THEY STAND   47

1. [Samuel Butler.] "Biographical Memoir of the late Samuel Taylor Coleridge." *The Analyst: A Quarterly Journal of Science, Literature, Natural History, and the Fine Arts.* London: Simpkin and Marshall. Vol. 1, No. 2 (September 1834): 148–52, and No.3 (October 1834): 22 (the latter signed S. Butler).

> Although published in London, the *Analyst* originated in the larger Shrewsbury area; hence Butler, as headmaster of Shrewsbury School, was publishing in the new local journal. STC's intention of becoming a Unitarian minister in the town was well known to other contributors to the present volume: e.g. Hazlitt of course, Wathen Call (items **2**, **3**), John Hughes Bransby (**35**), James Martineau (**29**), etc.
>
> Havens *Biblio* 1:78 notes that the first of these two contributions was reprinted in *Cambridge Chronicle* No.3758 (31 Oct 1834): 2, over the name B. Butler. I assume this is correct.

2. [Wathen Mark Wilks Call.] "Unpublished Letters written by Samuel Taylor Coleridge." *Westminster and Foreign Quarterly Review* new series 37 (1 April 1870): 341–64.

> Several letters published by Call were included in *Unpublished Letters of Samuel Taylor Coleridge* ed. E. L. Griggs (2 vols. London: Constable, 1933) and the full set of thirteen letters were published in *CL* vol. 4 STC also gave an annotated copy of *The Statesman's Manual* (1816) to Brabant. His comments on Edward Williams' *An Essay on the Equity of Divine Government, and the Sovereignty of Divine Grace* (1809) and "Modern (or Pseudo-) Calvinism," which Call quotes, are given in full in *SW&F* 1: 396–401.
>
> See the commentary in Chap. 5, "digging deeper."

3. [Wathen Mark Wilks Call.] "Unpublished Letters written by Samuel Taylor Coleridge in 1815–16." *Westminster and Foreign Quarterly Review* new series 38 (1 July 1870): 1–24.

4. [Nathaniel Langdon Frothingham.] "Notices of Recent Publications" [viz. joint review of *A Third Gallery of Portraits* by George Gilfillan, "Coleridge" on pp. 196–200, and of *Blackwood's Magazine* for February 1855 on "Revelations of a Showman" (viz. Barnum)]. *Christian Examiner* (Boston, MA) 58 (May 1855): 453–57.

> The author (1793–1890) was an American Unitarian minister and pastor of the First Church of Boston. His essay is a clever, sly undermining of Coleridge hero-worship. It reinforces the point made by the conjunction of the previous items from a different direction.

48   J. C. C. MAYS

The usual hand has written, then deleted with a question mark, "Xtian Examiner" in black pencil at the head of the article. The writer was apparently uncertain whether the notice appeared in the American *Christian Examiner* or the British *Christian Reformer*: see also items **18** and **20**.

5. [William Dougal Christie.] "Coleridge and Southey" [viz. review of Cottle *Reminiscences of Coleridge and Southey*], *Biographia Literaria* ed. Henry Nelson Coleridge and Sara Coleridge, and *Memoir of W. Taylor of Norwich*]. *Edinburgh Review* 87 (April 1848): 368–92. Reprinted in *Eclectic Magazine* (New York) 14 (1848): 195–208; and *Littell's Living Age* (Boston, MA) 17 (1848): 310–20.

The author (1816–1874) was a Cambridge Apostle, diplomat and man of letters. His review of biographical materials is made into a conspicuously conciliatory account of the STC-RS relationship—which is perhaps why it was placed in the volume at this point.

6. Anon. "Autographs, with Biographical Notices." *The Mirror* 5 (12 March 1825): 169–70.

7. Anon. "Samuel Taylor Coleridge." *The Churchman's Magazine* (New York), Vol. 2, No.36 (December 1855): 321–34.

An orthodox/episcopal church journal. Intelligent opening remarks of a general nature; thereafter a generous account of Coleridge's life; ending positively, with an assertion that his verse and philosophical writing are less important than his theological influence (quoting at the close "Dejection Ode" st.VI).

8. Z. "Memoirs of the Living Poets of Great Britain: Samuel Taylor Coleridge." *Imperial Magazine; or, Compendium of Religious, Moral, and Philosophical Knowledge* 4 (December 1822): 1094–1103.

A journal that advertised that it exists to maintain conservative standards. Coleridge was the third author to be discussed in the series, the first being Byron (in two articles, signed W) and the others (unsigned) being Southey and Moore.

Z summarizes the life of "this ingenious, but eccentric writer" waspishly. There are factual errors (e.g. STC in the Dragoons after Stowey, his Schiller translations after Malta) and the account tails away to end carelessly. Since it adds nothing but mistakes to the longer item (**7**) immediately preceding, one might ask why it is here? Or one might also ask, why was the preceding piece, published in 1855, positioned before this and the further (also unnecessary) piece (**9**)?

4 THE CONTENTS AS THEY STAND   49

9. W. "Memoir of Samuel Taylor Coleridge, Esq, with a Portrait." *New Monthly Magazine* 11 (1 April 1819): 240–43.

The portrait by Leslie is not included in present extract.

10. [Daniel Stuart.] "Anecdotes of the Poet Coleridge." *Gentleman's Magazine* new series 9 (May 1838): 485–92.

11. [Daniel Stuart.] "Newspaper Writings of the Poet Coleridge, and Letters to Mr. Stuart." *Gentleman's Magazine* new series 9 (June 1838): 577–90.

12. [Daniel Stuart.] "The late Mr. Coleridge the Poet, and Anecdotes." *Gentleman's Magazine* new series 10 (July 1838): 22–27.

13. [Daniel Stuart.] "The late Mr.Coleridge the Poet, and Anecdotes." *Gentleman's Magazine* new series 10 (August 1838): 124–28.

One might ask why so much from Daniel Stuart. Because the items came readily to hand? Or better, because they showed STC in a more realistic light than Henry Nelson Coleridge's *Table Talk* (1835) and Gillman's *Life* (1838)?

14. Charles and Mary Cowden Clarke "Recollection of Writers." *Gentleman's Magazine* new series 15 (September 1875): 323–327: viz. the latter half of a contribution beginning on page 316, where it is titled "Recollection of Writers Known to an Old Couple when Young... Part II.")

The Cowden Clarkes were joint-authors of *Recollections of Writers*, published in London and New York, 1878. See item **15**.

15. Charles and Mary Cowden Clarke "Recollection of Writers Known to an Old Couple when Young.... Part III." *Gentleman's Magazine* new series 15 (October 1875): 444–46; viz. the earlier, larger part of the contribution that ends on page 449.

This completes the previous contribution devoted to Coleridge. Were they together included as a comment on the obscured position of STC in the popular imagination? Or as an example of how time softens earlier memories?

16. Alice King. "Samuel Taylor Coleridge." *The Argosy* 40 (August 1885): 116–22.

50   J. C. C. MAYS

Alice King (1839–1894) was born and died at Cutcombe, Som. Although blind from the age of seven, she mastered seven languages and wrote using a typewriter. She was a prolific contributor to magazines and an author of fiction.

Like the previous two items, it is difficult to know why this one was included. Perhaps it is another example of popular froth, like the Cowden Clarkes before it. Alternatively, it could exemplify simple needs being adequately met, and one might note King's awareness that literary visitors to the Lime Street cottage marginalised Sara Fricker.

17. Charles F. Johnson. "Coleridge." *Temple Bar* 78 (September 1886): 35–54.

Reprinted in *Eclectic Magazine* (New York) 107 (1886): 776–90; and Johnson's *Three Americans and Three Englishmen*. New York: Thomas Whittaker, 1886. 41–87.

Academically efficient and frequently reprinted in its collected book-form up to recent years. A level of discussion in marked contrast to the preceding item (**16**), but placed in a way that leaves the question of relative value quite open.

18. [William Ware.] Review of *Confessions of an Inquiring Spirit* 1841 Boston edn. *Christian Examiner* (Boston and New York) 30 (March 1841): 121–25.

The author (1797–1852) graduated from Harvard, became a prominent Unitarian minister in New York and Massachusetts and wrote successful works of fiction and literary commentary. His review notes without comment that Coleridge rejects in emphatic terms the plenary inspiration of the scriptures and continues, approvingly, with lengthy quotations that support that position. He nevertheless closes by lamenting the "lumbering wordiness" and "sham profundity" that expose Coleridge to the charge of "literary mountebankism," and quotes as an example a paragraph on the "Pentad of Operative Christianity" as something that is unintelligible; however it is "printed or read, whether backwards, forwards, or in any other manner."

NB the journal-title is incorrectly given as the British Unitarian magazine *Christian Reformer* (in blue pencil) in the bound collection (same mistake as for item **20**, dated 1833).

19. Anon. Review of *Confessions of an Inquiring Spirit* 1849. *The English Review* 12 (December 1849): 247–71.

The first edition of *Confessions* was largely ignored by the reviews when it was first published, but it soon became a centre of controversy (see *S&F* 2: 1114–15). This second edition therefore came with an elaborate defensive surround, including an introduction by J. H. Green: Thompson *Cambridge Theology*. 86, 89–90 provides the context. The attack began in a review of J. C. Hare's edition of Sterling's *Essays and Tales* in the *English Review* (December 1848), under the title "Tendencies towards the Subversion of Faith." This was followed by Hare's riposte in *Thou shalt not bear false Witness against thy Neighbour* (London: Parker, 1849), which was in turn reviewed in a negative way by the *English Review* March 1849: this as prelude to the present attack on the second edition of STC's text. One must suppose the two reviews are conjoined to make a point about the virulent parochialism of the English journal and the (perhaps foolish?) openness to new ideas of the American one.

20. [Frederic Henry Hedge.] "Coleridge's Literary Character." Review of *Biographia Literaria* (New York, 1817), *Poetical Works* (London, 1829), *Aids to Reflection* ed. Marsh (Burlington, VT, 1829), *The Friend* (Burlington, VT, 1831). *Christian Examiner* (Boston, MA) 14 (March 1833): 108–29.

Hedge (1805–1890) was a New England Unitarian minister and founder of the Transcendental Club, a Germanist/Kantian and intimate of Emerson. His essay comprises an outside, long view which moves the argument onward from the preceding stalemate. The title is important because it uses the *Friend* and *Aids to Reflection* to argue that Coleridge is more of a littérateur than a philosopher. It acknowledges STCs general influence, but criticises his ability to handle theoretical argument. It expatiates at length on Kant, Fichte and Schelling *per se*, and was crucially influential on Emerson and Transcendentalism.

NB the journal-title is incorrectly given as the British Unitarian magazine *Christian Reformer* (in blue pencil) in the bound collection (same mistake as for item **18**, dated 1841; and see also item **4**.

21. [George Dyer.] Review of Coleridge's *Poems on Several Subjects* 1796. *Critical Review* 2nd series 17 (June 1796): 209–12. Reprinted in Jackson 1:34–35.

The earliest published piece in the collection. Perhaps included as a chance-discovered trophy item, but Dyer's early conversion to Unitarianism is possibly also relevant.

52   J. C. C. MAYS

22. [Thomas Moore?] Review of *Christabel etc.* 1816. *Edinburgh Review* 27 (September 1816): 58–67. Reprinted in Jackson. 1: 226–36.

23. Anon. Review of *Sibylline Leaves* 1817 and *Biographia Literaria* 1817. *British Critic* new series 8 (November 1817): 460–81. Reprinted in Jackson. 1: 355–75.

24. [Joseph Sortain.] Review of *Poetical Works* 1834. *British Critic* 16 (October 1834): 393–417.

> Sortain (1809–1860) was a Nonconformist minister and tutor in philosophy at Cheshunt College. He had a known interest in STC's writing and he reviewed for the High Church *British Critic*. These features separate this most interesting review of *PW* 1834, from a dissenting point of view, leaving other reviews of same title to follow as items **43** and **44**.

25. James Dykes Campbell. "Coleridge, Lamb, Leigh Hunt, and Others in 'The Poetical Register'." *Athenaeum* No.2994 (14 March 1885): 344–45.

> An odd piece of Campbell's to select for inclusion, but incorporated here simply as an example of his contribution to Coleridge studies, properly understood? Or could it be described as another, oblique comment on the limitations of Ashe's edition (for the other two reviews, which appeared later in the same year, see items **51** and **54**)?
>
> Three leaves matching the trimmed volume norm, filled recto and verso with a joined-up pasted-in cutting, narrow margins. The source is inscribed—in Greswell's loose hand?—at the close of the printed text.

26. Richard Garnett. "Letters from Coleridge to William Godwin." *Macmillan's Magazine* 9 (April 1864): 524–36. Reprinted in *Littell's Living Age* (Boston, MA) 3rd series 25 (1864): 275–85.

> Godwin, son of a dissenting (Sandemanian) minister, was educated at the radical new Hoxton Academy under Andrew Kippis. He was subsequently a rationalist atheist who became under STC's influence, a vague deist. Inserted here as a reminder of the catholicity of STC's friendships or of his unsound judgement?

27. [William Hazlitt.] "Coleridge's Lay-Sermon." Review of *The Statesman's Manual* 1816. *Edinburgh Review* 27 (December 1816): 444–59. Reprinted in Howe. 16:99–114; also Jackson. 1: 262–77.

Not to be confused with Hazlitt's three other—better-known—reviews of/ commentaries on the same text published in *The Examiner* on 8 September 1816, 29 December 1816 and 12 January 1817. These were afterwards collected in his *Political Essays, with Sketches of Public Characters*. London: William Hone, 1819. 118–24, 125–36, 137–39; reprinted in Howe. 7: 114–18, 119–28, 128–29.

28. [William Hazlitt, although probably extensively revised by Francis Jeffrey.] "Coleridge's Literary Life." Review of *Biographia Literaria* 1817. *Edinburgh Review* 28 (August 1817): 488–515. Reprinted in Howe. 16: 115–38; and Jackson. 1: 262–77.

29. [James Martineau.] "Personal Influences on our Present Theology: Newman-Coleridge-Carlisle." Review of eight titles by or relating to seven authors, including Coleridge's *Notes Theological, Political etc.* ed. Derwent Coleridge (Moxon 1853), the two latest titles being published in 1856. *National Review* 3 (1856): 449–94. Reprinted in his *Essays Philosophical and Theological*. 2 vols. Boston: William V. Spencer, 1866. 1: 329–405; and his *Essays, Reviews, and Addresses*. 4 vols. London: Longmans, Green, 1890–91. 1: 219–81.

See Chap. 1 on the marks on pages and Martineau's central place in the arrangement of Greswell's book, and Chaps. 5 and 6 on Martineau as a commentator on Coleridge. I add here that Greswell chose to reprint his thoughts on "The Late Sir Bartle Frere," from *Our South African Empire*, in *National Review* July 1884; also that, despite the closeness of Martineau and Coleridge on many significant matters, they differed fundamentally on the nature of Christian belief (see, e.g. below p. 90)

The pencil numbering at the head of the essay that reveals Greswell's concern for it to occupy a turning point in the volume. See also the unusual number of small pencil marks that indicate a very close reading.

30. Noah Porter. "Coleridge and his American Disciples." *Bibliotheca Sacra and Theological Review* (New York) 4 (February 1847): 117–72.

Porter (1811–1892) was a Congregational minister, academic philosopher, and became the eleventh president of Yale. He was the only author to be identified by name in the Contents list, and this is the longest essay in the volume. Aspects of STC's philosophical theology are praised but in the end critiqued for their exclusiveness and distance from the more direct and available American tradition.

54   J. C. C. MAYS

31. Anon. "Coleridge as a Theologian." Review of *The Friend* 1850, *Biographia Literaria* 1847, *Aids to Reflection* 2 vols. 1843, *Church and State* and *Lay Sermons* 1839, *Inquiring Spirit etc.* 1849, *Notes on English Divines* 2 vols. 1853. *British Quarterly Review* 19 (January 1854): 112–59.

32. John Tulloch. "Coleridge as a Spiritual Thinker." *Fortnightly Review* new series 37 (January 1885): 11–25. Reprinted in *Eclectic Magazine* (NY) 104 (1885): 305–15; *Littell's Living Age* (Boston, MA) 5th series 49 (1885): 557–66; and also in Jackson. 2: 156–74.

> Opens as a reply to, if not a review, of Traill's recently published volume and makes the same point as item **53** (and several other reviews not included by Greswell). Tulloch (1823–1886) was a liberal reformer in the Church of Scotland and Professor of Systematic Theology and Apologetics at St. Andrews. His *Movements of Religious Thought in Britain during the Nineteenth Century* was published later in 1885, with "Coleridge and his School" forming the subject of the first lecture/chapter. Meanwhile, later again, during the same year, Traill responded to this, the earlier essay, in "A Pious Legend Examined" *Fortnightly Review* new series 37 (1885): 223–33.

33. [James Frederick Ferrier.] "The Plagiarisms of S. T. Coleridge," *Blackwood's Edinburgh Magazine* 47 (March 1840): 287–99.

> Immediately summarised—and the severity of the charges deflected by arguing they apply only to Coleridge's writing—by Anon. "The Plagiarisms of S. T. C." *Knickerbocker Magazine* (New York) 15 (1840): 530–31.
>
> Ferrier (1808–1864) had already published essays on metaphysics in *Blackwood's*. He was a nephew of John Wilson: see item **44** above) and ended his life as Professor of Moral Philosophy at St. Andrews. He was sympathetic to German idealist philosophers and published on Berkeley, but appears not to have had a continuing interest in Coleridge. The charge of unacknowledged borrowing was not new, but the focus and directness of expression he gave it revived the matter as a central issue respecting Coleridge's originality and moral probity. This determined the way the family editors edited *Biographia Literaria* (2 vols. Pickering 1847), and how Kathleen Coburn set the editorial parameters of the Collected Coleridge (16 titles. Routledge and Princeton UP, 1969–2002).

34. Thomas Sergeant Perry. "German Influence in English Literature." *The Atlantic Monthly* (Boston, Mass.) 40 (August 1877): 129–47.

> T. S. Perry (1845–1928) was Lecturer in German and then in English at Harvard, a prolific essayist on a variety of authors (incl. Clough), translator

from French and German, and editor of the *North American Review* (1872–1874). The essay is an exemplary demonstration of informed, balanced American scholarship. Is it to be read together with item **33** as another conjunction of opposite evaluations, to Coleridge's advantage? Or taken as the best that could be said, which is still not enough?

Note that item **42** (on Doré's "Mariner") is a cut-and-paste from the January 1877 issue of the same journal.

35. James Hews Bransby. "Coleridge's Unitarianism." *Christian Reformer* 2nd series 1 (1834): 337–40.

Bransby (1783–1847) was a somewhat eccentric English Unitarian minister turned schoolmaster and author. Martineau (item **29**, page 472 fn.) refers to this item, which prints Coleridge's letter of January 1798 in which he withdrew from accepting the offer of the Shrewsbury meeting. Coleridge's Unitarian origins hover behind several items already included in the arrangement, so why this direct report here? To take us back to the beginning?

36. [Walter Pater.] "Coleridge's Writings." Review of Thomas Allsop *Letters & Recollections* [3rd edn., 1864]. *Westminster Review* new series 29 (January 1866): 106–32. Pater's first published essay, reprinted as

"Coleridge as a Theologian" in *Sketches and Reviews* ed. Albert Mordell (New York: Boni and Liveright, 1919). It was extensively revised and abbreviated, with the anti-Christian portions omitted, when it was combined with an introduction to Coleridge's poems taken from T. H. Ward's *English Poets* (1880) in *Appreciations* (London: Macmillan, 1889).

See Chaps. 5 and 7 for more on Pater.

37. Anon. "Coleridge's Table Talk." Review of *Table Talk*, 2 vols. 1835. *Eclectic Review* 3rd series 14 (August 1835): 135–40.

The *Eclectic Review* was a dissenting organ. It also took the side of J. C. Hare and John Sterling against the attacks of the *English Review* during 1848–1849 (Thompson *Cambridge Theology* 90–91).

38. [John Herman Merivale.] "Coleridge's Table Talk." Review of *Table Talk*, 2 vols. 1835. *Edinburgh Review* 61 (April 1835): 129–53. Reprinted in Jackson. 2: 27–55.

Merivale (1779–1844) was brought up a Presbyterian and later conformed to the Church of England.

39. [John Gibson Lockhart.] "Coleridge's Table-Talk." Review of *Table Talk*, 2 vols. 1835. *Quarterly Review* 53 (February 1835): 79–103.

40. Anon. "Table-Talk." Discussion of Luther, Selden, Lamb, STC and others (extract breaks off in mid-sentence). *Gentleman's Magazine* 202 (March 1857): 273–80.

> An opportunist insertion that broadens the interest of the items that precede it?

41. Anon. "Coleridge on Southey." Review of 3rd edn. of Robert Southey's *Life of Wesley*, 1846. *Christian Reformer* new series 3 (May 1847): 266–71.

42. Anon. Two pages of an omnibus review headed "Recent Literature" covering the *"Ancient Mariner"* illus. Doré (NY: Harper 1876). *The Atlantic Monthly* (Boston, Mass.) 39 (January 1877): 114–15 (out of a total number of pages appearing on 112–122).

> A joined-up cutting, narrow margins, pasted onto two blank leaves matching the trimmed volume norm, the recto and verso of the first leaf and the recto of the second leaf only (its verso blank). The source is inscribed—in Greswell's loose hand?—at the close of the printed text. The earliest of such inserted cut-and-paste items.

43. [Henry Nelson Coleridge.] "Coleridge's Poetical Works." Review of *Poetical Works*, 1834. *Quarterly Review* 52 (August 1834): 1–38. Partially reprinted in *Mirror* 24 (1834): 153–55; reprinted *Museum of Foreign Literature* (Philadelphia) 25 (1834): 560–76; also in Jackson. 1: 620–51.

> H. N. Coleridge played a large part in the assembling of this collection, adding many early poems and "correcting" the punctuation of the preceding, 1829 edition of *Poetical Works*. His argument makes a strong case for his uncle's originality.
>
> I note again that this review may have been rescued or stolen from a copy at the Bristol Central Library. It most likely represents an early stage of Greswell's Coleridge project.

44. [John Wilson.] "Coleridge's Poetical Works." Review of *Poetical Works*, 1834. *Blackwood's Edinburgh Magazine* 36 (October 1834): 542–70. Reprinted in Wilson's *Essays Critical and Imaginative*. 4 vols. Edinburgh: William Blackwood, 1857. 3: 293–343.

4 THE CONTENTS AS THEY STAND   57

Sympathetic, as if perhaps to make up for his earlier, insulting review of *Biographia Literaria* in *Blackwood's* and his passing remarks in his "Noctes Ambrosianae" in the same journal (September 1825 and April 1827). This and the previous conventional items prepare the way for the innovative claims made on Coleridge's behalf by Mozley in the item that follows this one.

45. [John Rickards Mozley.] "Coleridge as a Poet." Review of *Poems of Samuel Taylor Coleridge* ed. Derwent Coleridge and Sara Coleridge, 1854. *Quarterly Review* 125 (July 1868): 78–106. Reprinted in *Littell's Living Age* (Boston, MA) 4th series 10 (1868): 515–29.

Another example of a choice determined by Coleridge's larger set of interests. The Romantics (and what they lack) make up the introductory part of Mozley's argument, and this only becomes clear in an essay published the following year, where Coleridge is retrieved as the shaky foundation of a dilemma that became clearer at a later stage. The mature STC was as severe a critic of the Christianity of his time, as was Clough, and in addition, he continued to entertain some unorthodox beliefs, but he never doubted his membership of the main Anglican church. Perhaps that fact, in the face of people like Mozley, is why this item is included and why Greswell felt able to take orders at the time he finished completing his anthology. Its content points, in a wobbly way, to a judgement made outside it.

See Chaps. 5 and 6 for more on Mozley.

NB entitled (in near indecipherable black pencil) as ?British Quarterly, and perhaps also the numeral ?29.

46. [Margaret Oliphant.] "A Century of Great Poets, from 1750 downwards: No. IV—Samuel Taylor Coleridge." *Blackwood's Magazine* 110 (November 1871): 552–76. Reprinted in *Littell's Living Age* (Boston, MA) 4th series 23 (1871): 643–61; *Eclectic Magazine* (New York) new series 15 (1872): 138–57.

A prolific popular author and regular contributor to *Blackwood's*. Her essay earns its place here by lowering discussion to a level more appropriate to Coleridge's achievement.

47. Anon. "Coleridge's Lectures." Review of *Seven Lectures etc.* ed. J. Payne Collier. *Gentleman's Magazine* 202 (February 1857): 158–64.

A defence of a publication that had come under attack from other reviewers.

58   J. C. C. MAYS

48. Mortimer Collins. "Coleridge's Country." *Belgravia* 2nd series 2 (1870): 197–203

Reprinted in *Eclectic Magazine* (NY) new series 1 (1870): 621–25; and *Pen Sketches by a Vanished Hand.* 2 vols. London: Richard Bentley and Son, 1879. 2: 108–20.

The earliest venture into reading Coleridge as a Quantock poet? The author, a Plymouth man, was a colourful personality; he is celebrated in T. H. S. Escott's *Platform, Press, Politics, and Play.* Bristol: J. W. Arrowsmith[, 1895]. 271–73

49. Anon. "Early Spring on the Quantocks." *Saturday Review* 4 April 1885: 440–49.

This item is more obviously a celebration of Wordsworth and of Kilve: Coleridge is only mentioned once and then as Wordsworth's collaborator when the "Ancient Mariner" was conceived. The author writes as a seasoned traveller, with experience of the Peak District, Helvellyn and Dartmoor, the Lake District and the Alps, yet also of the route from Alfoxton House to the sea (see Dorothy Wordsworth *Journals* 4 April 1798 and Pamela Woof's gloss on Pardlestone Lane, down past Kilve Mill, etc.). The author makes a show of local knowledge in all seasons and the omission of smuggling may be deliberate; in its place, the introduction of the Stowey gypsies at the close is indeed Wordsworthian.

I often wonder if William Greswell might have written this piece. In his first book on the neighbourhood, he called the lane "one of the most romantic little pathways in the land of Quantock" (page 6; and see also 158–61), and it is glued to a specially treasured piece of paper. One might also remark that, in 1915, he had in mind to leave his Kilve house called Aldenham to the nation to commemorate Wordsworth's attachment to the place. See below Chap. 6. Alternatively, if not Greswell, then most obviously William Luke Nichols.

Three leaves matching the trimmed volume norm, filled recto and verso (last verso blank) with a joined-up pasted-in cutting, wide margins. The first leaf carries the blind stamp of Dunnill, Palmer and Co. of Manchester, apparently dating from the 1860s or before. The source is inscribed—in Greswell's careful hand?—at the close of the printed text.

50. Helen Zimmern. "Coleridge Marginalia: Hitherto Unpublished." *Blackwood's Magazine* 131 (January 1882): 107–25. Reprinted in *Littell's Living Age* (Boston, MA) 152 (1882): 356–69.

This—along with items **17** and **34**—is notable for displaying formal academic standards that contrast with the many appreciative essays on Coleridge's writing.

51. Anon. "The Aldine Edition of Coleridge." Review of *Poetical Works of Samuel Taylor Coleridge* ed. T. Ashe. *Spectator* No.2981 (15 August 1885): 1076–77.

Mainly negative: the new edition adds nothing that supplements Coleridge's achievement and much that muddles it.

Two leaves matching the trimmed volume norm filled recto and verso with a joined-up pasted-in cutting, wide margins. The source is inserted—in Greswell's careful hand?—at the close of the printed text.

52. Anon. "Mr. Russell Lowell on Coleridge." *Standard* 8 May 1885.

Lowell's address on the Thorneycroft bust in Westminster Abbey. For Lowell and Coleridge, see *Coleridge's American Disciples* 31 etc.

Three leaves matching the trimmed volume norm, on which is pasted (recto and verso, the last verso blank) a joined-up cutting, narrow margins. The source is unusually in Greswell's loose hand, employing blue pencil, above the printed title on the first leaf.

The attribution to the *Standard* may be incorrect. An article with same headline under the same date appeared in the London *Times* No.31441, page 4.

53. Anon. Review of H. D. Traill *Coleridge* [Macmillan, 1884].

The review is of the London, not the New York edition (which is from another publisher), and could date from 1885. It comments on the distortion caused by ignoring Coleridge's Christian thinking and reading him simply as a "man of letters."

Two pieces neatly trimmed and pasted from a journal with wide margins onto the recto of a single leaf matching the size of the trimmed norm. Source not given and not traced. NB the small pencil markings on the printed text similar to those that appear, plentifully, in the Martineau review (item **29**, dated 1856).

54. T. Hall Caine. "Notes on Coleridge" [review of T. Ashe's edition]. *Athenaeum* No.3011 (11 July 1885): 48–49.

Mainly negative as far as Ashe's edition is concerned, claiming that what the notes add may be reckoned small beer.

Three leaves matching the trimmed volume norm, filled recto and verso with a joined-up pasted-in cutting, narrow margins. The source is inscribed—in Greswell's loose hand?—at the close of the printed text.

∗ ∗ ∗

55. A. L. H. [Arthur Lee Humphreys]. "Gleanings after Time, no. XXII. Stowey Friendships." The source is not given, but London *Antiquary* ran a series bearing the first line of the title during the period 1885–1890.

Humphreys (1865–1946) was a native of Wellington, Somerset, and manager of Hatchard's Bookshop, Piccadilly. He was the author of fifty books, including several on the local history of his county, and subscribed to Greswell's *Land of Quantock* (1903).

Two leaves of small "Dodington Rectory" notepaper, filled recto and verso with a joined-up pasted-in cutting, narrow margins. Source not given. The item is the first of five pasted onto Dodington Rectory paper (viz. items **55–59**). The weekly contributions probably date from circa 1885 or 1886).

56. A. L. H. [Arthur Lee Humphreys]. "Gleanings after Time, no. XXIII. Stowey Friendships (Continued)."

Two leaves of small "Dodington Rectory" notepaper, filled recto and verso with a joined-up pasted-in cutting, narrow margins. Source not given and not traced.

57. A. L. H. [Arthur Lee Humphreys]. "Gleanings after Time, no. XXIV. Stowey Friendships (Concluded)."

Refers familiarly to William Luke Nichols revising his *Quantocks and their Associations* (pub.1873) at Woodlands House, and see **49** above on the very knowledgeable piece published anonymously in 1885. Nichols died in September 1889 and the second edition of his *Quantocks* appeared in 1891.

Two leaves of small "Dodington Rectory" notepaper, filled recto and verso with a joined-up pasted-in cutting, narrow margins. Source not given and not traced.

4 THE CONTENTS AS THEY STAND 61

58. Anon. "Samuel Taylor Coleridge's Cottage at Nether Stowey. Interesting proceedings."

This dates from after the cottage plaque-event, which took place on Friday afternoon, 9 June 1893, and so perhaps from Monday, 12 June 1893. David Miall *The Wordsworth Circle* 22 (Winter 1991), 82–88 notes that William Greswell wrote to the London *Telegraph* as early as 9 September 1892 under the name of "Wayfarer" to suggest a campaign to acquire the cottage for the village and perhaps the nation. Greswell published over his first and last initials "Coleridge and Nether Stowey" in *Athenaeum* No.3425 (17 June 1893): 765–66. The same day he wrote a letter to James Dykes Campbell—now at the Humanities Research Center in Austin Texas—outlining the course of action that was eventually followed: "We must save the place from the Brewers!!" For Hon. Stephen Coleridge's photograph of the cottage with the new plaque above (as here: not as now beside) the door, see *Letters* ed. EHC (1895) facing 1: 214.

Four leaves of small "Dodington Rectory" notepaper, filled recto and verso (the last verso blank) with a joined-up pasted-in newspaper cutting, narrow margins.

59. Anon. "Mr. Russell Lowell on Coleridge's Works."

The opening sentence refers to the unveiling of the Westminster Abbey bust as having taken place "yesterday," which would have been 7 May 1885. See item **52** above.

Three leaves of small "Dodington Rectory" notepaper, beginning on the verso of item **58** and continuing recto and verso with a joined-up pasted-in newspaper cutting, narrow margins. Source not given and not traced. NB this is the fifth and last item pasted onto small "Dodington Rectory" notepaper inserted at the rear of the already bound volume.

CHAPTER 5

Greswell the Compiler

Abstract A return to the editor or author: why did he turn to Coleridge in the first place? It was an odd, late starting-point in the 1870s and 1880s, but perhaps it is explained by his background. He came from a family of achieving clerics (that is, except for his elderly father). He was educated at a new, experimental school in Bath, where he made friends who would help him find a place to publish in later years; he went on to get a modest degree at Brasenose College Oxford. He made friends with, perhaps coached, young rebels like Edmond Holmes at St. John's and Richard Boodle at Magdalen; and, after an interval, he went to teach in South Africa and to return a few years later to take orders and to publish a book which took a stand in supporting Sir Bartle Frere, the ex-governor who had been sacrificed to political expediency. He published a good deal through the next decade on South Africa and other matters—including essays on Wordsworth and Coleridge and general fauna and flora—until he gave it up in 1903.

To return to the collection of Coleridge articles, it is noteworthy, as one gets to know it, how severe the critique of Coleridge is. From the very beginning, it is clear that Greswell was intent on displaying him as deeply duplicitous; and he sets Coleridge up as a fraud from the moment the latter abandoned his plan of becoming a dissenting minister to accept a bursary from the Wedgwood brothers. He repeated the claim that Coleridge was a fraud that was given fresh impetus by Carlyle in 1851 and had stained Coleridge's reputation as a serious thinker immeasurably by the end of the

© The Author(s), under exclusive license to Springer Nature Switzerland AG 2023

J. C. C. Mays, *Coleridge in William Greswell's Workbook*, https://doi.org/10.1007/978-3-031-38593-3_5

63

64   J. C. C. MAYS

century. It was only challenged seriously by the poets (Dante Gabriel Rosetti, Swinburne, the poets of the 1990s) whom Greswell does not include, and Pater and Mozley whom he does (Greswell's nos. **36** and **45**). James Martineau's essay precedes them (no. **29**), of course, and it is the most clever and most ambiguous of this group of three. It gives an unsurpassed summary of Coleridge's achievement, which Greswell studied with much attention, and it dismisses Coleridge because the latter could only say "Try It"—the proof that failed Wathen Call, Sterling and many others. It was a proof that looks more than suspiciously like that of the godless Cantabridgeans—like Grote, Sidgwick, Seeley and others. Does one trace the hand of the more radical Boodle here?

Keywords Greswell's early life • His family background • His early education and at Oxford • Then teaching in South Africa and making-up his mind • A severe and definite judgement concerning Coleridge?

1   EARLY YEARS

Coleridge was an odd—or better, very specific—choice to learn theological probity from in the 1870s, and one wonders how far the task he represented was imposed on Greswell and how far accidental. Whatever the case, it led to the book that is the subject of the present one and to the twisted, unexpected lesson it eventually produces. The book summarised what Coleridge could teach him and what Coleridge could not, in short order. And there Greswell left the matter, and got on with the rest of his life.

The background story begins with his grandfather, who is perhaps still known today and who died when our protagonist was five years old. William Parr Greswell (1765–1854) had been presented to the incumbency of Denton near Manchester in 1791 by the first Earl of Wilton, to whose son he was tutor. He developed the school and was rector there for sixty-two years. Five of his seven sons went to Oxford and won high honours: Clement, William, Edward, Richard and Francis. The two other sons were Charles, a medical man, and Thomas Hearner Greswell, master of Chetham's Hospital, Manchester. His publications meanwhile ranged widely, from Pico della Mirandula to Parisian typography to writing original verse, and his large library was sold at Sotheby's in February 1855.

Greswell's father was his second son, again named William Parr Greswell. He was born at Denton in 1796, went to Manchester Grammar School, matriculated at Brasenose College Oxford on 31 March 1814, aged 17, was a scholar 1815–1817, became B.A. in 1818, then was a fellow of Balliol from 1818 to 1838. And from 1837 to 76 he was rector of a North Somerset college living, Kilve-cum-Stringston, until his death on 6 November 1876, aged 80. He published *A Commentary on the Order for the Burial of the Dead, Considered as a Manual of Doctrine and Consolation to Christians* (2 vols. Oxford 1836); and was a subscriber to the *Works of William Laud* (7 vols. in 9. Oxford 1847–1860). He married Mary Ann Harrison, who was born in Manchester, when he retired in 1838 and when she was twenty. The couple had ten children during the following twenty years.

William Henry Parr Greswell (1848–1923) was their fifth child and eldest son. He was baptised at Kilve on 15 May 1848: his father was then fifty-one years old, two years younger than Coleridge's father when Coleridge was born. Little is known about his childhood: he enjoyed messing about in boats and nearly drowned, he was given a copy of the Routledge Wordsworth sometime after 1862 by his eldest sister, Agnes. He attended Somersetshire College Bath, and won a lot of book prizes (which he kept), although it was the sort of select school where everyone won prizes. He matriculated at Brasenose on 24 May 1866, aged just 18. He was a scholar during 1866–1869, and proceeded to the BA in 1871 and the MA in 1873. He went to South Africa shortly before his father died, became an Anglican deacon in 1883 and a priest in 1885 (Bath and Wells). He returned from South Africa, meanwhile, was curate of Aisholt from 1884 to 1889 and was rector of Dodington from 1888 to 1913 (in the gift of Sir Alexander B. P. Fuller-Acland), where the population in 1881 was ninety-one. He married a local woman, Blanche Carew, in 1895, but there was no issue. He died in 1923, aged 74, and was buried at Bicknoller.

I will just add for the record the known details of young William's two brothers. Charles Herbert Greswell was born 28 June 1852 and baptised at Kilve 25 July 1852. He became a civil engineer and worked in India and Ceylon, where he met and married Edith Tatham in 1881. They returned to England with their three young children in 1891 and his wife died in 1913. He owned the tea-producing estate of Avisawella in Ceylon from 1898 to 1922, and, following his retirement, lived at Holford, Clifton and Bicknoller. He died in 1926, and was the father of, among others, the famous Somerset and England cricketer, Bill Greswell (1889–1971). The second brother, Arthur Edward Greswell, was baptised at Kilve 29 January 1860. He matriculated at Merton College Oxford, 14 October 1879, and proceeded to BA in 1883, MA in 1886. He married Evelyn Blathwayt (born at Chumleigh, 21 June 1878) in 1904, and they had three children (all girls). He died in 1931, aged 71.

Such are the known facts, and what surrounds many of them must remain speculation. William Greswell III's education at the new, liberal, Somersetshire College in Bath surely made an impression. The main school building he attended was at No.11, The Circus, which had originally been owned by William Pitt the Elder. It became a school in 1858, very much on the example of Rugby, and the premises reverted to being a private home in 1886. During the time Greswell was there, about a hundred boys from all over the country were prepared for university or the army. They claimed the advantage of a good staff-student ratio and boasted of winning university prizes. The school concentrated on classics and mathematics, but geography and history were also taught. A succession of once-famous chess-players taught maths: Edmund Pierpoint and Edward Thorold while Greswell was there, and William Pollock after he left. Alexander Bell taught there for the year following Greswell's departure in 1866, which one might take to illustrate its open and adventurous spirit. The founding headmaster, Hay Sweet Escott, retired in 1873 and succeeded Greswell's father as rector of Kilve, following the latter's death. W. L. Courtney (1850–1928), who followed two years behind Greswell as a pupil, filled in as headmaster for the three-year interval following the older Escott's death. Meanwhile, another pupil—Thomas Hay Sweet Escott, son of the founding headmaster—after becoming a lecturer at King's College London and editor of the *Fortnightly Review* from 1882–1886—retired and, after an interval, was replaced at the *Fortnightly* (from 1894 to 1928) by Courtney.

The fact of being at such a school at such a time surely affected the young Greswell. Thomas Hay Sweet Escott described him as "a former schoolfellow and present friend,... an accomplished writer for the periodical press, as also an Oxford scholar of repute" (*Platform, Press, Etc.* 102). W. L. Courtney was either more objective or more impatient, but Greswell must have been aware of his later philosophical standing at New College Oxford. Greswell was to publish essays in the *Fortnightly Review* fifteen or so years after he left Bath and, at the least, his earlier contacts with editors like Escott and Courtney must have helped him. At the same time, as the younger Escott also notes (p. 101), Greswell's father was the only brother in his family who failed to take a "double first," and "was held, therefore, by his relatives to have discredited his name, and is fabled to have received remonstrances on his indifference to study." If young Greswell attended the school having inherited such a frame of mind, it might have acted as a kind of suppressant-cum-encouragement. He was obviously liked, but there is no evidence that he distinguished himself academically.

2   OXFORD

Greswell was a Hulme Exhibitioner at Brasenose from 1866 to 1869. It was no great honour at that time but he spent the money on books—theological (e.g. F. D. Maurice and Drs. Pusey and Butler), literary (e.g. Scott and Milton, more Wordsworth and Carlyle), and miscellaneous (on insects and ferns)—which he again retained to the end of his days. There are indeed a good many such acquisitions, and it looks as if he made a conscious effort to catch up on the debate that occupied the English church in the 1830s and 1840s, as well as its recent standing. They possibly distracted him from study because his degree results were undistinguished: a second class in Mods, a third class in Greats. Perhaps the result did not particularly bother him: the list of his books made in 1917–1918 records a large album he won as a prize for athletics at Brasenose in 1868, containing photographs of himself. Then, five years after taking his degree, some of them spent in London, he became a lecturer in Classics and English literature under the Higher Education Act of the Cape Legislature, from 1876 to 1884. This gave him the title of professor at one of the four Cape colleges at a salary of £200 a year, where he taught and also examined students for their degree. (The Cape system was based upon the system that then pertained at the University of London.)

His uncles at Oxford, Edward and Richard, were both prominent figures during his time there. Edward, who had matriculated at Brasenose in April 1815, the year after Greswell's father, moved across to Corpus Christi where he became known as "Old Harmony." His books on the chronology of the Bible and on the principles and arrangement of the Gospels became standard texts; and, on behalf of the Tractarians, he took on R. D. Hampden and William Colenso. He was the author of some thirty titles in the Bodleian catalogue, before he died in his college rooms at the close of William Greswell's third year (29 June 1869). Greswell's other uncle Richard had gone straight to Worcester College in 1818, where he stayed until he retired. He married a rich heiress, which made it possible for him to support many University and other causes. For example, he supported the National Society for Promoting Religious Education (as opposed to the non-denominational British and Foreign School Society); he was an early and continuous ally of Gladstone; he rose first to oppose the Darwinian theory of evolution in the famous Oxford exchange between William Wilberforce and Thomas Huxley in July 1860; and he was one of the founders of the Ashmolean Society. He died in the year Greswell graduated (1871), but he taught his two daughters Hebrew. Joanna, who produced her book, *Grammatical Analysis of the Hebrew Psalter* in 1873, died in 1906; Helen lived on at 70, Woodstock Road, and continued to subscribe to multiple copies of the books that Greswell published until she died in 1913.

Oxford at the time Greswell was an undergraduate was in a tumultuous state. Pusey and Liddon were at Christ Church; Jowett, J. R. Green and Matthew Arnold were at Balliol. His relations favoured the moderate conservatives, he himself was not necessarily on the side of "Mr. Kidglove Cocksure" (Robert Bridges' term for Arnold): there was controversy everywhere. Mrs. Ward attended John Wordsworth's first Bampton Lecture in March 1881 and, as I said earlier, the seeds of *Robert Elsmere* were sown (*Writer's Recollections* 1: 222–26). She wrote her novel looking for the "forward strain," the "world ahead" rather than the world in process of being left behind, to bring us to theism with Christ as a model of character but without belief in the miraculous part of Christianity. The best-known provocateur at Brasenose at the same time was Walter Pater, who was a fellow of the college. His first, anonymous journal publication on Coleridge had been published in 1866 (item **36**); and the conclusion to his essay, when it was included in his first book-publication, *The Renaissance* (1873), was borrowed from his earlier (1868) essay on William Morris in the *Westminster Review*. This caused consternation in Oxford and not least in his own college. As I said, Greswell's reaction to such events is not known, but he cannot have been unaware of them and I believe they worked their effect on him.

The person who assembled Greswell's book must likewise have been conscious of others who had charted the main areas of theological discussion he inherited, up to the moment in the 1870s and 1880s, when he felt the need to settle his own position. Given Greswell's connection was with Oxford, it would have been natural to pick up with Arnold and Jowett and those on the liberal side of the debate that had exploded with *Essays and*

Reviews (1860). If he took any notice of Cambridge matters, it would have centred on the debate surrounding the anonymously published *Ecce Homo* (1865), whose author became quickly known as John Seeley. However, although several contributors to *Essays and Reviews* mentioned Coleridge with respect, he did not figure prominently in the Oxford debate that followed. And, at the same time, he remained more central in the Cambridge tradition that included not only Seeley but also F. D. Maurice (who strongly disapproved of the Oxford book: Ellis 250–51) and Grote, Sidgwick, Marshall and others. The Oxford background of English nineteenth-century liberal theology was Latitudinarian; in Cambridge, it was Rationalist and Utilitarian. By an odd twist, it would appear, from what the compiler excludes as much as what he includes, that the Oxford situation of High Church reaction describes what Greswell wanted to escape and, in this respect, the situation articulated in Cambridge was more to his taste.

The two Greswell uncles were prominent fellows of Oxford colleges during at least some of the time he was an undergraduate and, while the family would certainly have balked at Bentham, the other great seminal mind they might have allowed—Coleridge—was a less dangerous person from whom to learn. In this way, an extremely well-connected, theologically conservative family might have assisted a young man to assemble a diverse range of material, while he read and finally re-arranged it to tell a slightly different story. The Coleridge project might have been suggested by anyone, and one can easily imagine any of the brothers being consulted over questions arising from the furore over Pater's first (anonymous) journal publication (item **36**) or first book-publication, *The Renaissance* (1873). If a family member was involved, this would explain the presence, in Greswell's book, of paper salvaged from a book-order to a defunct Manchester bookseller (see above Chap. 2). One can imagine the advice: why not take your tutor's *Westminster Review* essay on Coleridge, who is a poet you have always liked, set it against other essays on Coleridge—many of which deal with his ideas, and his theology in particular—and work out what he is saying and who is correct?

As far as I know, Greswell never commented outright on the figures that distinguish his Coleridge selection—I mean, not his tutor Pater, nor James Martineau, nor Mozley—nor did he collect their writings. One must nevertheless suppose that a project that aimed to bring together sample commentary on Coleridge's writing in all its forms, beginning with the decades in which he was alive, would lead to an understanding of the historical process: a widening of sympathy, a damping down of extreme positions. It might even encourage its maker to take a spectatorial position with respect to the issues involved. If that is how it proceeded, it was completed in a way that took a stand, although you would hardly know it. It delivers a decisive verdict disguised as a muddle; or put another way, an indecisive verdict that exactly fits the bill.

Greswell appears not to have made any lasting friends in his undergraduate years at college but, oddly, he appears to have made lifelong friends after he became BA with at least one younger contemporary and maybe more. It is not known what he did during the interval between graduating (1871) and going to the Cape in 1876, but it would be reasonable to assume that he took on students, to read with them during that time (as, for example, his schoolmate Thomas Hay Sweet Escott had done). What other way to explain his friendship with Edmond Holmes and Richard Boodle, at St John's and Magdalen respectively, who graduated after him and both subscribed to *The Land of Quantock* in 1903. Boodle indeed remained a lifelong friend, who subscribed to all Greswell's publications until he unexpectedly died in 1918. The friendships are important because Holmes, who became an inspector of schools, published radically "progressive" and "child-centred" positions as soon as he was free to do so; and Boodle, who emigrated at about the same time Greswell left for the Cape, articulated his religious position very clearly soon after he arrived in Canada. This will be made clearer in the following chapter.

There is one other detail to settle. Greswell took up his post in South Africa a few months before his father died on 6 November 1876. The Classics master and Cape University "professor" at Bishop's College, O. A. Hogarth, had died suddenly in the February of that year, and perhaps Thomas Hay Sweet Escott (who had also been at Queen's, like Hogarth) put in a word on Greswell's behalf. One must suppose the elder William Greswell's death came suddenly and the situation was awkward. Whatever the case, the younger Greswell travelled to replace the much-lamented Hogarth on board the USS "European" in June 1876, purchasing two books on Napoleon at a stopover at St. Helena en route.

The spirit in which Greswell left England can only be guessed at. One does not know when he bought the large number of theological books he owned. A good many of them were purchased with scholarship money in earlier years in an effort to catch up: to read himself into the theological situation where he found himself. Others must have been purchased as he spoke with the likes of Holmes and Boodle. He selected earlier titles—Pusey and Wilberforce, for example—but likewise, on the other side, Mark Pattison and Brooke Westcott. He registered Seeley's *Expansion of England* as "a most important vol: of Essays" when it appeared, but he did not possess a copy of the same author's earlier *Ecce Homo* or *Natural Religion*. He became a freemason at Oxford, in 1869, and, while his circle of acquaintance was wide, he appears not to have read William Hale White as one might have expected. There is absolutely no suggestion that he felt challenged by the questions that confronted, for example, Tennyson in a fundamental way (Lyell and Chambers), or George Eliot (the text of the Bible, Strauss, etc.). His position was not in relation to belief itself, but to how to believe. This is how things were by the 1870s–1880s, when earlier theological difficulties were differently assimilated.

In other words, a large part of what caused a commotion when the Oxford *Essays and Reviews* was published in 1860 was taken for granted by the 1880s. Thus accommodated, Greswell's collection is a retrospective view of the difficulties in a familiar scene. Non-progression is an integral part of the argument, and indeed one begins to realise why the second half of the collection as a whole repeats the point the first half has already made, albeit in a different way. So Matthew Arnold in *Literature and Dogma* describes a sort of "natural Christianity," spiritual but not credal, demythologised but not exactly (in Arnold's sense) "cultured." The Arnoldian position is already acculturalised for Greswell: it amounts to a spiritual feeling more associated with a living landscape than a high cultural ideal. One might also add that Arnold was a little Paterised by Greswell. The latter takes over Martineau's critique of the Platonic Coleridge and develops in a way closer to Pater (see the Pater article, p. 127). In the end, Coleridge is found as a magic poet and a poet of place. He simply deserves to be memorialised—saved from the brewers!—as if he was something like a Quantock Mona Lisa.

3   After Oxford

I noted the extended close of the period of Greswell's book: the principle of selection loosens in late 1870s-early 1880s, and ends with Thorneycroft's 1885 bust (item **52**), and a single American essay from September 1886 (item **17**). This overlaps a period of growing overseas political opportunities brought about by W. E. Forster (1875), Seeley's *Expansion* (1883) and the Westminster Conference (1884), after which the new hopes began to stall. In poetry, it matches the direction prompted by Dante Gabriel Rossetti and Swinburne: the renewed appreciation of Coleridge's lyricism.

The original binding took place after 1886, and the final Dodington Rectory inserts were incorporated during 1886–1893. If the project emerged from a mild crisis of conscience, any crisis appears to have become even less pressing, less relevant during these later years. The final arrangement—perhaps fifteen years after beginning—even suggests that the book's beginnings might have been left behind because they then proved burdensome. The present book is not mentioned in the final list Greswell completed in January 1918, unless it is "A book of Press Cuttings (W. Greswell)" on the bottom shelves of the mahogany bookcase. If it also ended as a drift towards Unitarianism, Greswell walked away in a mood that found questions of dogma irrelevant. He travelled to the Cape and quickly found himself involved with different, practical issues of the moment that had little to do with insoluble questions. The first essay he wrote for *The Cape Monthly Magazine* (in December 1876) was "The Poetry of Nature from a Greek and Modern point of view." The next, in August 1878, was "A Short Study of Wordsworth." He returned to England in 1883, still adding to his earlier project, and eventually had it bound so that the book could remain closed. It commemorates a throwing-off, a coming into his own, a realisation that he already possessed what he wanted, which was self-reliance.

The part played by the project in Greswell's affairs is not least important in the way it was shed. It was overtaken in the later 1870s-early 1880s by a possibly unexpected opportunity, although the manner in which he departed left minor inconsistencies in the record. He was elected to the Royal Colonial Institute on 5 March 1882, after being proposed (in his absence?) by T. Watson and seconded by W. Torbet (a South African name), and the Institute *Proceedings* register him as most active there in 1883–1885 and in 1889–1894. (He remained a member until his death.) He then became deacon and curate of Aisholt in 1884 and the delayed fact appears to cement his future.

It is true that Greswell's decision to move abroad might not have been quite as sudden as it now appears. As I said before, history and geography were taught at Somersetshire College and Greswell agreed on their importance (see *South African Empire* 1: 276). People close to him moved large distances. His brother removed himself to Ceylon; Arthur Blake, a neighbour from Padnoller, sailed to Cape Town (*British Mail* 2 May 1881) and subsequently subscribed to *The Land of Quantock*; Boodle removed to

Canada. It appears to me unlikely that Greswell went abroad with publishing thoughts of confederation in his head. But the tangible excitement of living in a far larger new world—where the main problems appeared as other peoples' and the problems of the congested old world were far distant—played its part. As Greswell makes clear at once, in his *Cape*-chapter on Froude, he writes after the events in which Froude had meddled: the subject of confederation as far as it applies to South Africa had been interfered with to the extent that it could not happen as soon as might have been hoped (ibid 1: 216). In this way, the bungled opportunity left the way clearer for Greswell to be more emphatic in describing the task and its problems, both inherent and introduced by Westminster incompetence. Sir Bartle Frere—imported from India and abandoned in Africa to fail without home support—is discovered as Greswell's luckless hero. Greswell presents him as like Coleridge's Alexander Ball: just, decisive, and honourable. He was the exemplary English gentleman who re-embodied the simple values of Thomas Arnold after *Tom Brown's School Days* had made them a joke. Put another way, *Our South African Empire* is a defence of the best Greswell knew against what the world does to it: its hero is an honourable statesman like that of Coleridge's "Complaint and Reply" (quoted and discussed by Lockhart item **39**, Mozley item **45**, and Johnson item **17** in Greswell's book), who is trapped by a situation not his doing. It is as if, by some sleight of hand and unjustly, Frere became the unhappy Coleridge, Froude and others his Carlyle, and there was no way out but to press on. All Greswell's early hopes were expressed in his requiem, which covered both men.

One might now judge that Greswell showed multiple prejudices—on behalf of colonisation and against the Dutch and the Germans, in particular—but he was less concerned with idealities than practical obstacles to progress in the particular here and now. His thoughts on how Greek was wasted on a Kafir student at the close of the second volume provides another example, although his notions of a secular education would surely have been put by Coleridge in a different way. Greswell wrote as one newly looking for compromise in a foreign situation that was not his own; final principles—made clear in the elegy on Frere—are set on one side. He communicates the intricacy of a conflicted muddle very well—at least, as far as the fresh eyes of a young British contemporary could be expected to see them. Missionaries and conversion, native polygamy and silence over Bishop Colenso (whom Uncle Edward had specifically challenged), are presented as he, and not his family members, saw them. If Greswell escaped to Africa to clear his mind of the issues that dogged him in England, it was a success. The discussion represented by the Coleridge materials must have appeared sterile and narrow compared to the situation he met there. They involved issues of how Western Europe needed to interact with the world beyond.

Our South African Empire and Greswell's early essays were written with a sense of release and discovery. His unique perspective was his live report of how Westminster policy and interventions did not connect with the reality on the ground: were causing more harm than good. As time went on, he lost touch with the changing situation and found himself writing at other people's request and school textbooks for money. The situation advanced, the English political situation changed, and confederation was no longer the topic of the 1890s as Africa advanced towards the larger miseries of the Second Zulu War. The opportunity to write textbooks and essays became simply opportunist and, after twenty years, Greswell withdrew from the field. He was still, in 1907, remembered as a possible contributor to the Cambridge *Modern History* at a time when suitable authors were still scarce, but he was either passed over or he declined (Ingram 10). He left things to go their own way, as he had left the Coleridge essays in the second half of his collection dangling. In the end they point in directions the compiler did not follow. He had learned his lesson and his further aims were modest. He turned away from Coleridge, nearly, to cultivate his own garden: the Quantocks, their past history and their present beauty. He spent the remainder of his life in a far distant, still agricultural parish and, in words borrowed from the close of William Hale White/Mark Hutchinson's novel, *Catharine Furze* (1893), his sermons were probably of the simplest kind: "exhortations to pity, consideration, gentleness, and counsels as to the common duties of life. He spent much of his time in visiting his parishioners and in helping them in their difficulties."

CHAPTER 6

The Unwritten Script

Abstract This chapter returns to Greswell's life after he returned from South Africa, believing for a while in federation but soon loosening that hope as events on the ground advanced, and he settled into married life as rector of Dodington (north-west of Nether Stowey). While the book may be read in a way that sees the later half confirm the message of the earlier part, it might be read as slyly doing the reverse: a turning of the first half on its head. As I said, the ostensible plot is stated in items nos. **1–17**; and then repeated over again somehow differently.

At the same time, you might notice that the Unitarian ideal has a special place. It changed a great deal in England before and in Coleridge's day, and nowhere more obviously than in the United States. The extracts taken from American journals occupy unique—nay, privileged—positions in Greswell's argument: they separate what they consider the chaff from the real article, whether the topic is his theology at large or his table talk or marginalia. And my point is that Martineau's essay (no. **29**) launches one into this context: it is different from the context of earlier chapters, where Dr Brabant and the Rosehill Circle set the scene. It connects James Martineau with the Cambridge circle, all of whom found Coleridge's "mysticism" too mystical. Pater makes the same point—choosing to pretend his essay is a review of Thomas Allsop's *Letters and Reflections* (no. **36**), which was strongly suppressed by the Coleridge family. And in Mozley's essay, too (no.**45**), which sets up Coleridge as a poet of unfettered intellectual ambition in contrast to Wordsworth. In many ways,

© The Author(s), under exclusive license to Springer Nature Switzerland AG 2023
J. C. C. Mays, *Coleridge in William Greswell's Workbook*,
https://doi.org/10.1007/978-3-031-38593-3_6

75

76   J. C. C. MAYS

however much of Greswell's choice of essays might have owed to others (in particular, to his friend Boodle), they select themselves to make an argument that owes much to the "other place" (viz. Cambridge)

Keywords A closer look at Greswell's return to England • Is Coleridge really set aside? The essays by James Martineau, Pater and Mozley • Are they there only to humour Greswell's Oxford friend and likely contributor, Boodle?

1   DIGGING DEEPER

My earlier chapters were intended to provide a guide to what one first meets in Greswell's book: to supply a loose narrative to hold onto. But now, forget chronology and attend to the thematic counterpointing of separate arguments about Coleridge that emerged during his lifetime, and were repeated and developed during the decades that followed. Then notice that these same arguments are taken in new directions in some lengthy essays dating from the 1850s and 1860s; that the focus loosens in the choices from the 1870s; and that the whole comes to a stop with an admixture of anodyne or unrewarding discussion from the 1880s. The previous chapter was intended to supply the biographical background of the compiler and to explain why I suggested he undertook his project while he pondered ordination in the Church of England. Prompted by whatever reason, reactions to and debate about Coleridge became the means through which he considered the issues involved.

The present chapter probes further if only because the form the project took as it waited to be bound is highly unusual, if not unique. Others beside Greswell had turned to Coleridge for spiritual guidance from the 1820s onward, but they did not frame their effort in the same way: solely through reviews of and essays about Coleridge's publications across a span of so many years, long after he died. As I have explained, it is most helpful to connect the periodicals with the ideals that inspired their beginnings and consequent editorial standpoint; and it likewise helps to identify the anonymous authors, despite Greswell's lesser interest in them. Of course, his book was put together for a private purpose, and he had no need to give additional reasons for what he was doing. The key to his method lies in the way in which an author, Coleridge, is repeatedly assessed by how his writing was received and used, because this unlocks the question of whether he delivered on promises made to groups and individuals who held different ideas and beliefs. The grounds of Greswell's expectations are not made explicit—that is, there is no evidence that he was ever anything but an orthodox member of the Church of England—but he shows a surprising interest in the views of others at variance with his supposed position.

His book is thereby more than a comprehensive collection of Coleridge criticism. Successive items interact in ways that promote and subtract from meanings one first takes at face value. The accumulating sense of non-progression is an integral part of the argument, until one begins to realise the second half of the assemblage repeats the point that has been already made in a different way. The whole turns out to be a record of Coleridge's usefulness to one retrospective reader at a time when changing life-values came momentarily to rest and began to move in a different direction: a moment for an Oxford graduate when, after *Essays and Reviews* had been published, people began to recognize the foundations of their faith had shifted, while others in the established church clung more tightly to the High Churchmanship represented by *Lux Mundi*. The story that emerges from Greswell's patchwork is of a particular intellectual legacy marked largely by failure, all the time leaving hints of an exciting future that nevertheless remained a promise. Both sides of the story are represented with equal justice, and Greswell erred on the side of prudence when he came to a decision. His patchwork nevertheless contains—or better say, *barely* contains—a vivid sense of the alternative options. The four items at the beginning of the series exemplify the discordance beneath the bland historical record. Unfolded, they reveal the problem that frames everything that follows in the second half of the series: pointers to solutions that stand outside the frame.

The opening two-stage contribution by Samuel Butler (item 1) is superficially innocent. For reasons given later, it was important for Greswell to open with an overview that connected with Shrewsbury, where Butler (Coleridge's earlier rival for the Craven Prize in his second year at Cambridge) had made himself famous as the headmaster of Shrewsbury School. Butler's fond memories were written for a mainly local readership, but they necessarily leave a gap in the knowledge of Coleridge's middle-life that provides the reason for continuing the sequence with letters written in 1815–1816 from Calne in Wiltshire (items 2 and 3). These again look innocent on first sight—Coleridge engaged in intellectual discussion of theological matters arising from a book lent to a local doctor, Robert

Brabant (1781?–1866), who practiced in Bath. However, many readers would know by the time the letters were published (1870) that Brabant became a core member of the freethinking "Rosehill Circle" at Coventry, headed by Caroline Bray (née Brabant) and including, besides Brabant, his older and learned daughter Rufa (properly Elizabeth Rebecca), who began a translation of David Strauss' *Das Leben Jesu* which was completed by Mary Ann Evans/George Eliot. They might also have known that in 1843, Rufa married Charles Hennell (1809–1850), who in 1838 had published his *Inquiry concerning the Origin of Christianity* that accidentally reflected much of what Strauss had written and anticipated what Coleridge's executors were to publish posthumously in *Inquiring Spirit* (1841, 2nd ed. 1849); or again that Robert Brabant introduced Hennell's book to Strauss, who in turn arranged for its translation into German in 1839.

More is thereby involved than bringing forward letters to fill a chronological gap in Butler's eulogy. One must take seriously the commentary surrounding the published letters describing the dialogue between Coleridge and Brabant over Richard Field's *Of the Church* (1635). They describe an attempt at persuasion on Coleridge's part that failed, much to the approval of the person bringing forward the letters. One needs to read this against an essay on Montaigne in which John Sterling deplored the influence of Coleridge and his followers in persuading him to take clerical orders that he (Sterling) afterwards came to regret in the same radical journal, the *Westminster Review* for July 1838. Carlyle repeated and embroidered the same point in the famous Chapter 8 of his *Life of Sterling* (1851): how the spell Coleridge cast over his followers was a kind of entrapment,[1] which in the present case, Brabant was able to resist. And then, besides, by the time Greswell assembled his book, a large enough circle that included remnants of the Rosehill Circle like the American Moncure Daniel Conway, and Coleridgeans like James Dykes Campbell, knew very well that the anonymous person who submitted the letters to the *Westminster* suffered the same fate as Sterling.

---

[1] Carlyle's wife wrote to her brother, John:, in the year following its first publication: "None of Mr. C's Books have sold with such rapidity as this one. If he would write *a Novel* we should become as rich as—Dickens! 'And what should we do *then?* ' Dee and do nocht ava!'" *New Letters and Memorials of Jane Welsh Carlyle* ed. Alexander Carlyle (2 vols. London: John Lane, 1903), 2: 35.

This person was Wathen Call (1817–1890) who married Rufa (Brabant) Hennell, seven years after her first husband's death. Moncure Conway described Call as "almost a reappearance of Sterling" and how, after much hesitation he had been persuaded by his reading in "Mr. Smooth-it-away Coleridge" to take orders in the Anglican church (*Autobiography* 2: 140). And how, after his ordination in 1843, and a further period of even more anguished soul-searching, he resigned from his orders in 1856. Call published his own version of the story in the second edition of his verse collection, *Reverberations* (1876), where the subtitle reads "*To which is prefixed THE GROWTH OF OPINION WHICH MADE ME LEAVE THE CHURCH.*" In the later 1880s, Call invited Ernest Hartley Coleridge to lunch and made the full set of letters available to be published, while humbly allowing that the grandson might "prefer not to be personally acquainted" with him (Walters nos.168–73). The grandson's edition of the *Letters* in two volumes 1895 included only a few of the letters published by Call, and Call's bitterness at having been misled by the older Coleridge lies behind his concurrence with Carlyle's verdict in phrases like "the unconscious insincerity of the philosophical theologian" in his *Westminster* commentary (item **3**, p. 17).

The above, or a good part of it, must have been in Greswell's mind when he placed the letters to Brabant where he did, accompanied by Call's commentary, following Butler's innocently conventional praise. With all their ramifications, they explode every concession to Coleridge's authority as a spiritual leader that was ever made. The next item in the series (no. **4**) by an American Unitarian minister, is couched as a review of three miscellaneous books and pretends to a lighter tone, but it repeats the process of demolition. It cleverly and slyly undermines the hero-worship of Coleridge by comparing him to P. T. Barnum, celebrated for his hoaxes which he justified on the principle of "I don't believe in duping the public, but I believe in first attracting them and then pleasing them." A medley of diverse items then follows this opening salvo, as if deliberately to half-bury a theme that has been too obviously stated. After what comes before, in the way I have explained, item **5** is too obviously diplomatic, item **6** is evidence of becoming a simple collector's item, item **7** is an example of over-benevolent kindness, item **8** is a case of gross ignorance, and so on. I have supplied brief suggestions how the items progress in Chap. 4, and I repeat that items **16** and **17** appear to close the opening section in a larger sense of grouping by linking together popular and professional estimations of Coleridge's poetry. Each is excellent in its way: both are unlikely to mislead (deceive) their audiences. This anticipates the way the entire collection is to conclude, with more faith in Coleridge the poet than in Coleridge the theologian. Again, I have added comments on the items that follow item **18** et al in Chap. 4.

2 THE IDEAS INVOLVED

I remarked before how many items in the book connect in some way with Unitarianism: the connection between Shrewsbury in the journal that contains item **1** is aligned with Coleridge's withdrawal from accepting the offer of the Shrewsbury Unitarian meeting in January 1798, spelled out clearly in item **35**. James Martineau—in item **29** (p. 472 footnote), published thirty-two years later—makes clear that the connection and the withdrawal from a difficult job into an easier means of support were not forgotten. Then again, besides the many Unitarian authors and journals that are drawn upon—American as well as English—consider again items **2** and **3**: the letters written at Calne. The town has a long history of non-conformity and the Presbyterian congregation became Unitarian after 1770. Anyone with an acquaintance with Joseph Priestley would know that he wrote some of his most ambitious philosophical works while he lived in the town (from 1773 to 1780), working as librarian for the Earl of Shelburne.

Unitarianism changed a great deal in the hundred years after Priestley's day. Its connection with revolutionary politics declined. It had long begun to absorb a critical view of the foundation texts on which orthodox Christianity rested, in advance of the furore over the same that erupted with the English translation of *Das Leben Jesu* (1846). The Socinian connection diminished, and for the most part it became an undogmatic, flourishing branch of the Dissenting church, even though it left many outside it puzzled as it to what it was that it worshipped. James Martineau (1805–1900) articulated its position most intelligently in nineteenth-century Britain and was also highly respected in America, where he had important connections. It is intriguing to see how much easier it was for him then to follow the route previously trodden by Coleridge: throwing off the shackles of Necessitarianism, studying Kant and the German Idealists, making the idea of conscience the foundation of his ethical beliefs. He and Coleridge shared the same approach to many theological questions: the fundamental public difference, of course, being the relation between church and state (subject of the book that Greswell notably omitted, in his choice of reviews), which again loosened in many important ways during the course of the century. The theological difference is more subtle and, in the present context, more important. It involves the nature of conscience, which, for Coleridge, is differently balanced between human need and God's presence. Unfortunately, Martineau's doctrinal views became at length too radical for the majority of Unitarians of his time and, despite the positions of influence he reached, he nowadays attracts less interest than his sister, Harriet, or his philosophical opponent, Henry Sidgwick.

The relationship between Martineau and Coleridge might be described as close but of a kind that Martineau felt compelled to maintain at a distance. The title of his 1856 essay (item **29**)—"Personal Influences on our Present Theology"—is important because it is as much to do with a context of feeling as with philosophical argument. It sandwiches Coleridge between Newman and Carlyle as it moves from the erstwhile new theology of the Tractarians and Newman (Oxford), to the later philosophical reaction of Coleridge and F. D. Maurice (Cambridge), to the literary reaction across the period emblematized by Carlyle's earlier and later writings (Scotland and London). The summaries and criticisms of each of the three chosen authors are acute and nicely balanced, and Martineau is so generous (tactful) to each of them that the element of reserve in his remarks on Coleridge in particular is difficult at first to pin down. So, Newman's pursuit of logical argument is seen as evading the prior necessity of founding faith on conscience, and thus coincident with the "Oxford" practice of professing a creed in order to believe it: "*Believe* first, and *conviction* will follow" (item **29**, pp. 464–66). Carlyle, too, finding the idea of the divine in everything, made the supernatural natural and ended in despair: hope reduced to scorn (pp. 483, 485, 488). Coleridge and Maurice meanwhile—although categorized among the philosophical Cantabridgeans—are also described as "*believing men*" (p. 483). The phrase is not just a reference to Coleridge's "most believing mind" in "Frost at Midnight": it describes a spiritual enthusiasm that can run ahead of critical judgment and unwittingly led its followers into a swamp. The Cambridge school that Martineau found more profitable to engage with—despite equal difficulties in accepting all they stood for—were figures like Sidgwick, Seeley and Mozley. The recommendation Coleridge made in *Aids to Reflection* to "TRY IT" (Aphorisms on Spiritual Religion VII: *AR* 202) was too close to the message poor Wathen Call had listened to, to his bitter regret. Despite Martineau's respect and sympathy, and the excitement his cogent summary conveys, Coleridge is set on one side as a personal influence and a warning to the cause he served. It needs to be read alongside Martineau's reply to Tyndall's Belfast Address in the *Contemporary Review* ("Modern Materialism: Its Attitude towards Theology," reprinted in *Essays and Reviews* 4: 197–267) to realise how deeply he identified with part of Coleridge's position, despite his qualification that Coleridge was too mystical. One might indeed pause and say that his overall judgement was fair at the time, and that it had to be while so much of Coleridge's later writing remained unpublished.

The essay by the foremost Unitarian philosopher of his day occupies a pivotal position in the arrangement of Greswell's book, and it is one of three lengthy essays by contemporary English thinkers that give the latter half of the volume its distinctive flavour. The earlier part develops the depressing argument about Coleridge promising more than he delivers, repeatedly in changing contexts, the American view being generally more discriminating simply because it is detached. Then Martineau's lucid condensation and critique launches the book positively into its later half, despite its subtly contrived qualification. It allows the remaining reviews and essays to muddle towards a close with lesser expectations resting on a broader mix. In such a context, the contributions by Pater and Mozley resonate with—are isolated by—the same kind of intellectual excitement, beyond the self-destructive Carlyle

Moving onward to Pater's essay (**36**)—retitled "Coleridge as a Theologian" when it was reprinted, unrevised, following Pater's death— one might wonder why such a novel interpretation of Coleridge's aesthetics should pretend to be a review of Allsop's *Letters and Recollections*: specifically, of the third edition published by Farrah in 1864 (actually a re-issue of the second, 1858 edition, with a new Preface), twenty-eight years after the first. Pater must be reckoned to have deliberately chosen Allsop (1795–1880) because of his connection with radical politics and anti-clerical causes: in particular, he had been seriously involved in Orsini's attempt to assassinate Napoleon III on 14 January 1858. The Preface to the "new" 1864 edition challenges all those conservative religionists— Coleridge's family editors along with anyone who would suppress what was most alive in Coleridge—and, at the end of his introduction, Allsop defiantly quotes John Moultrie's sonnet "To the Anonymous Editor of Coleridge's Letters." As I said before, Pater was a teaching fellow of the college of which Greswell became a junior member, and he had already begun to transgress convention before this, his first print-publication. One could argue that Greswell inserted the essay—a distortion of Coleridge's thinking as far as it relates to Coleridge—to point up the misleading use to which Coleridge might be put. This is possible, but I will suggest another explanation in the next section of this chapter.

Last of the three, Mozley's essay (**45**) was written by an important figure in nineteenth-century intellectual life who moved from High Anglican beginnings to a kind of deism. He was—as I have said before—a nephew of the two very different Newman brothers besides being a Cambridge Apostle and friend of Grote, Sidgwick, Seeley and others. The reference in his first paragraph to "a late edition" of Coleridge's poems refers to Sara Coleridge's Preface to the 1852 edition (repeated in 1854, 1860 and 1863), where she excuses herself for excluding later poems because they are "of not more than an ephemeral interest." Mozley's argument sets up Coleridge as a poet of unfettered intellectual ambition, whose failure to achieve a proper resolution is testament to his integrity: this, in comparison in different ways, to Wordsworth, Byron and Shelley, the first two of whom literally "sold out." This argument on behalf of a more ambitious kind of intellectual poetry is more satisfactorily pursued in Mozley's companion-review of later nineteenth-century poets that he published in the same journal the following year; where Clough emerges as the hero who expresses a similar philosophical-theological predicament when engaging with transcendental values. Mozley's earlier essay fails because the examples of Coleridge's later poems that he cites are unconvincing, and this may be the point. This apologist for Coleridge also cannot deliver what he claims.

However, one must not forget that Mozley's essay was numbered tentatively in pencil as "29": that is, as an alternative to Martineau's essay at the centre of the volume. How can this be? In what way could one replace the other at the turning point? The only answer I can give is that Greswell had in mind the Unitarian Christian background that Martineau represented and, less obviously, what it shared with Mozley and Mozley's intellectual companions. Religious views on final matters had converged to become a loose kind of undogmatic deism in the course of the century. Seeley's "Natural Religion" is only a tad less self-contradictory than Carlyle's "Natural Supernaturalism" (the title of Chapter 8, Book 3, of *Sartor Resartus*): at least, he held it to be so. And while Greswell may have included Pater's essay simply as a silent counterblast to Arnold, whose publications through the 1870s went out of their way to deprecate dissenters, he may well have found the context of discussion in Cambridge more persuasive and invigorating: a welcome breath of fresh air.

3   AND THE UPSHOT (FOR GRESWELL)

The Oxford world in which Greswell moved during the decade following 1866 was very different from the decade following his father's departure from Oxford thirty years before. The later times were troubled in a different way: the issues involved looked less outwardly dramatic but were equally complicated, as old ties loosened and the concept of natural religion was more easily, more widely accepted. In the present chapter, I have described Greswell's collection as if it was contrived to confirm Carlyle's assertion that Coleridge was a false leader. And yet at the same time, the collection retains an equal interest in a Unitarian context that carries Greswell into a different future, where the Coleridge connection serves a different purpose. It is true that Martineau is silent concerning fundamental differences over theological points, that Pater bends Coleridge's thinking too obviously to support his own claims, and that Mozley's essay is relatively unknown because his reading of the too-few poems he cites has convinced nobody. Against this, consider Mozley's essay against the Carlylean argument Greswell contemplated. Mozley sets up Coleridge as a poet of unfettered ambition whose failure to achieve an intellectual resolution testifies to his utter integrity. His Coleridge looks forward through different eyes from Carlyle's, who gets lost in a fog. And it is no accident that Mozley, Seeley and company represent a clear line of thinking outside the Oxford circles of Jowett and Matthew Arnold that Greswell was educated in.

It is as if Greswell, following John Morley ten years earlier in another Oxford college (Lincoln), had picked up John Stuart Mill's essay on Coleridge and been reminded of a kind of truth that Carlyle traduced but did not extinguish. Some sort of residual truth remained in Coleridge's poetry for Greswell that other disappointments could not destroy. Even if the flame flickered, it could be hinting at more than the peacemaker knew. If this is what the inclusion of Mozley's essay is intended to register—linking as it does with the more difficult points in Martineau's analysis that Greswell read over so carefully—it is useful to set it beside the analysis of Greswell's Oxford contemporary Boodle, which was more clearly set out.

The sequence of essays Boodle contributed to the Toronto *Canadian Monthly* from June 1879 onwards display an organised mind mapping itself onto an English intellectual world emerging from upheaval. He read Tennyson's *Idylls of the King* as an evolving sequence that reflects the slow death of romance, that is, as the inevitable disintegration of culturally manufactured religious bonds. He wrote of Mallock's *New Republic*—published in book form in 1877, following publication in journal form in 1876, and circulating before that in manuscript form in Oxford university circles—as a parody of the personalities and ideas he knew intimately. He presents Mallock himself as a grotesque retro-Catholic: his own position being, although he was the son of a Somerset parson, acidulously rational.

Boodle's religious views emerge, soon after he moved to Montreal around 1880, in a pair of essays published in an American journal under the shared title, "A Study in the Growth of Scientific Morality." The first essay reviews the religious history of the previous thirty years—"years of utterance on all sides," "the crisis of the revolution of thought"—and the close of Pater's *Studies in the History of the Renaissance* (1873) is cited among other texts alongside the claim that the time has come for reconstruction. The second essay suggests that the way forward is John Seeley's *Natural Religion* (1882), which Boodle summarises and discusses at length. On the first page of the first essay (p. 511), he writes of "Carlyle's 'Life of John Sterling' [sc. as] revealing the hollowness of Coleridge's religious compromises." In the second essay, he argues that "the writer [Seeley] is clearly himself a believer in supernaturalism, if not as very tangible, yet as an underlying possibility" (p. 606):

> the minimum basis of a faith without a personal God and without miracles, is a compromise honestly offered by one who himself apparently still cherishes these beliefs. (p. 607)

The discussion ends with quotations from Leslie Stephen and Aristotle, and an acknowledgement of the persistence of the supernatural, the unknowable in an age of science, as a kind of aspirant humanism: "as far as possible to think the thoughts of immortals, and to live in our every act up to the noblest part within us" (closing words on p. 615).

Boodle thus emerges as an Oxford contemporary and lifelong close friend of Greswell who left a record of wide reading and conclusions to be drawn from it that appear to have been close to Greswell's, although more definitely "advanced," and Greswell never articulated his own views so firmly. One might even speculate that Boodle left his mark on the final arrangement of Greswell's book—which might be said to make a strong case for a more radical argument than the first half of the book allows—although I think this unlikely. Greswell was certainly indebted to Seeley's views on imperial federation, which many have argued were consonant or connected with Seeley's views on the church. Seeley was led repeatedly to insist, following the anonymous publication of both his *Ecce Homo* (1865) and *Natural Religion* (1882) that, while modern religion needs to reject its early supernaturalism, its development should not end in secularisation: that he remained a member of the Anglican church in good faith. Greswell made a more explicit commitment to the same church through ordination as a minister, leaving his thoughts on controversial matters unknown. His conclusion appears to have been that, while Coleridge often failed to deliver all he pretended, this was not sufficient reason to forego the hope of leading an ordinary (orthodox) Christian life.

Of course, like Martineau as cited above, neither Carlyle, Seeley or Greswell was aware of all that Coleridge really did deliver, since it was not available until the last volume of the Bollingen Collected Coleridge was published (the *Opus Maximum* in 2002). I will return to this final twist of events in Chap. 8.

CHAPTER 7

Greswell After Coleridge

Abstract A return to Greswell, describing his life after the South Africa experience. He held Frere to have been a man of honour, betrayed by those he though were his friends. Conditions in Africa changed, and Greswell also changed his mind—although not his adherence to Frere. He accepted that conditions in Canada, say, were more appropriate to his earlier views on colonial expansion, and wrote short books on such related topics until he stopped writing them altogether. He turned towards publishing books by subscription on local history. They went into considerable detail but were based on Greswell's own qualifications, which derived from a close knowledge of the whole county of Somerset mixed with a quantity of historical romance. They remain outside the main course of dependable history books that will never lose their value but they contain odd thoughts to dwell over—like, for instance, Alfred's manipulation of his forces according to the water-levels in the River Parrret and its many tributaries.

Greswell resigned his ministry at Dodington because of his wife's illness and moved to Minehead at the end of the century's first decade. He had meanwhile, earlier than or soon after he abandoned his Coleridge project, assumed the position of Secretary to the newly founded Coleridge Society. He acted as its Secretary and was active in reporting the local scene to Ernest Hartley Coleridge until the Cottage was purchased by the National Trust. He regretted that it could not contain a Wordsworth and Coleridge library and privately dreamed of a rival scheme at Aldenham, nearer to

© The Author(s), under exclusive license to Springer Nature Switzerland AG 2023

J. C. C. Mays, *Coleridge in William Greswell's Workbook*, https://doi.org/10.1007/978-3-031-38593-3_7

87

88   J. C. C. MAYS

where he had been brought up. He died exactly a century ago, shortly after his last Somerset book was published, and was buried at Bicknoller.

Keywords Greswell's later life • Governor Frere in the South Africa book • Greswell's views on colonialism modified as conditions changed • His turn towards writing books on Somerset local history • He subsequently becomes the man on the spot in the appeal to save the Coleridge Cottage • Resignation from holy orders due to wife's illness • Dreams of a Wordsworth library at Kilve, where he spent his early years

1   COLONIAL FEDERATION

The plan of Greswell's South Africa book is simple. It moves from the early Dutch and the English settlements, to the two kinds of native races and the Kafir wars, then to the two Dutch republics, the South African federation and the failed Frere administration, and thereafter tumbles to a close. The question Greswell asked of Bartle Frere was the same he had asked of Coleridge. Did he deliver on his promise? Was he a man of honour? Greswell's answer is that Frere was prevented from delivering what he was able to do by confused and contradictory instructions from London. Greswell blames Carnarvon, Froude and his Uncle Richard's old friend and hero, Gladstone. His book turns on Frere's fate, although it keeps the idea of federation alive and the later chapters silently carry the theme as an unanswered question.

In April 1896, Greswell wrote a letter to the younger Molteno, his former pupil at Bishops, thanking him for his recent book, *A Federal South Africa*, and politely but frankly still disagreeing with it. Molteno regarded Frere as the wrong man for the job: his previous administrative experience with only subject-races, in a hurry, an agent of British colonial policy, and therefore "useless for good in South Africa." Molteno was right and Greswell wrong, but the difference did not matter by then.[1] The pattern on the ground was changing, the Second Boer War began in 1899 and continued until 1902. Africa was never a state as simple as Canada or Australia were to prove, in that its native inhabitants were a tangible force in their own right and also because the Dutch had arrived there first.

---

[1] Greswell persisted in his view. He wrote apropos Molteno's book in his late catalogue of books: "He began with great promise, but sank gradually in a quagmire of Scotch Radicalism of the 'dour & narrow' type."

However, it is noticeable that when Greswell published his *Geography of Africa South of the Zambesi* in 1892, he referred to his first South Africa book as "written, as it were, with bated breath" (page vi) because words and phrases like "Empire" and "Imperial control" could not at that time be mentioned. His views on federation underwent a sea-change and, in the *Outlines of British Colonisation* in 1893, he went back and around to give an entirely different, "lighter" history. There is no talk either of federation or of the Frere debacle. Its short chapter on a South African empire takes a completely new approach that leaves open the way the configuration might work out

In a way, the muddle in which Greswell found himself in South Africa—writing about a country that was less suitable only than Ireland or India as a candidate for colonial expansion—was his liberation. He was able to turn to other examples—in Canada and Australia, but also in the West Indies and further east—in Mauritius, the Eastern Archipelago and Hong Kong—to illustrate his thesis at a later time. He then returned to South Africa to probe isolated issues: for example, the problems raised by competing groups of settlers, like the Dutch or Germans, or the accommodation of native people into the master plan. He put to use his work on Coleridge in British journals to multiply the appearance of his production: by first writing articles on colonisation and federation, then mixing these with essays on Wordsworth and Coleridge in the Quantocks, and eventually reaching out to touch on special subjects like nature pure and simple. Volume 2 of Sidney Mendelssohn's *South African Bibliography* (2: 741, 795 and 843) lists twenty further examples of his writing on various aspects of the Cape in magazines like *Murray's Magazine, Good Words, Empire Review* and *Leisure Hour*, the latest dating from 1903. Indeed, one might reckon he was his best while writing on place and its fauna and flora. It is indeed why he was pigeonholed as a writer on scientific subjects in the official South African record.[2]

All told, Greswell made his mark by the fortuitous conjunction of his visit to South Africa coinciding with the date of Seeley's *Expansion of England*, published in completed book-form in 1883. It is no surprise that his essay won the essay-prize for the best essay on imperial federation in 1887, though he was no better than Seeley in suggesting how federation

---

[2] See Cornelis Plug., "Greswell, Reverend William Henry Parr (geography, ornithology)." *S2A3 Biographical Database of Southern African Science.* Online at <https://www.s2a3.org.za/bio/Biograph_final.php?serial=1145> accessed 7 July 2018.

might be incorporated into the English legal structure. At no earlier time could he have claimed that the journey between London and South Africa would take only eighteen or twenty days (*South Africa* 1: 49, ibid 1: 91): a fact that indeed makes it just possible for him to have visited home once or twice during his allotted span of "seven or eight years" abroad. His own apology is sufficient for what followed thereafter. It occurs in a letter now at Texas written on 16 September 1912, when he reminisces about his years at Dodington Rectory: those "somewhat strenuous times when I had to supplement the somewhat exiguous stipend of a rector with literary contributions to newspapers & magazine—most of it rubbish, I fear—..." And he went on to note a reference to his writing on Canada in a recent issue of the *Fortnightly* that praised him. "I begin to look upon my lengthening shadow with respect elongated beyond proportion in autumnal days." He knew that his writing on colonial topics was done within limits that he did not stray outside. His later anxiety about foreign interests is apparent, and he withdrew from the field when he had said all he knew.

2   LAND OF QUANTOCK

By the time Greswell retired from publishing in national journals in 1903, he had shifted his focus entirely. He had begun to publish in the *Proceedings of the Somersetshire Archaeological and Natural History Society* in 1897, and continued to do so regularly up to 1911; thereafter, he published only two more articles in 1920. More importantly, he published a series of five monographs by subscription between 1903 and 1910, and then revisited the first with a rewriting of the same general theme in *Dumnonia and the Valley of the Parret* from the same publisher in 1922, shortly before he died. All the books were written on an ambitious scale and their pattern was set at the beginning. He walked the ground, they were based on detailed research and investigation, but they were inspired by love and only incidentally on an disinterested search for knowledge. The result was a completely different kind of history-book from, for example, Chadwyck Healey's *History of the Part of West Somerset, etc.* (1901) or Edward MacDermot's *History of the Forest of Exmoor* (1911, 1973), both of which have retained their historical value. Greswell's earliest, *The Land of Quantock*, was based upon what he knew and was useful in moving him afterwards to fill in the gaps; the last, written quickly in his remaining few years, *Dumnonia*, shifted idiosyncratically eastwards and expressed the heart of what he knew.

His final book came closer to what he wanted most to say than any other. It was centred on Alfred and the Vikings, describing how Alfred's men could outwit the invaders at their own game. He had already described how the ideal English virtues were embodied by Bartle Frere and Admiral Blake (the latter in a monograph published in 1907). Now the main scene of action centres on Kings Arthur and Alfred. W. T. Reeder praised his suggestion that the Danish chieftain Hubba was slain at Combwich and not at Appledore (in Devon), and that Alfred's decisive victory over Guthrum was at the Somerset and not the Wiltshire Edington. I have no opinion on the matter and can say only that his argument makes an odd contrast to a modern archaeologist's concept of Dumnonia, which covers a much larger area, extending from the two peninsulas of south-west Britain and southern Wales into Britanny, and having as much to do with the early church as with Alfred's battles.[3] At all events, Greswell's descriptive and historical account becomes a part-mythical retrospect. There are of course links with the earlier writing. For instance, in describing his Admiral Blake publication to Francis Cheetham, he talks of "these degenerate days" and how the great admiral displayed "Patriotism and Religion." In the Dumnonian book, he begins with a map that writes the name across the short stretch of land that stretches westward from the Quantocks to the border with Devon and anecdotally disposes of any further pretensions to the title. His interest moves instead to the oddly rising tides in the Parret—as he says, "the real opening to the interior of Somerset" (p. 23)—and there it remains, with the sea and rivers central. When he completed this, his last book, he had done: Alfred, the great sailor, its hero; the Celtic Arthur assimilated into his Saxon successor.

Greswell stopped writing in 1911 before his final resurgence at the end of the decade. At the same time, he also had to resign his ministry at Dodington in order to move his ill wife to Martlet House, Minehead. As his late letters to Ernest Hartley Coleridge show, it was a great wrench for him to leave the old neighbourhood—yet "There was nothing else to be done"—and he continued to worry over the Cottage. "You have summed up exactly the feeling, locally, ... The villagers have regarded it simply as 'a mine of gold' and Moore [the previous owner] himself, civil as he is, always has a rankling grievance that he did not get more from it" (letter dated 25 October 1912). He lambasted the lack of local support, he

---

[3] As an example, I cite Susan Pearce, *The Kingdom of Dumnonia: Studies in History and Tradition in South-Western Britain, A.D. 350-1150.* Padstow, Cornwall: Lodenek Press, 1978.

hoped from the beginning that the project might be expanded to house a local library, and he still hoped to keep in touch with it all. His very last letter to Ernest Coleridge, dated 18 September 1915, describes his attempt to revive Aldenham—the farmhouse in Kilve that he had purchased—as a separate, self-maintaining enterprise to house his books, and leave it to the National Trust to be run somehow in conjunction with the Coleridge Cottage. It was a noble thought, but it obviously failed.

He nevertheless finished his *Dunmonia* and was buried at Bicknoller, where his brother Charles lived. It is a village situated to the west of the main tourist route. His wife chose, when she died much later, to be buried at Crowcombe, three miles away, where she originally came from, alongside her father.

3   THE STOWEY COTTAGE

Greswell's later writing on the Quantocks played its part in the emerging local history of the area, as the interaction with it by writers like Albany Major proves, but the single most lasting result of his local researches was one that he appears to have been divided over. This was the part he played in the recovery of the Coleridge cottage at Stowey, to guide it into the safe keeping of the National Trust. He would most probably have liked to think that his writing on colonialism was of its time, concerning a great missed opportunity; and that what he did in applying himself to local history was useful, too, in explaining how the contours of the landscape contributed to its historical shaping. He left no trace of what he thought about the consequences of his early Coleridge project—it was a private part of his growing-up, and he just turned his back on it—but it left him in a position he could not ignore when the time came. He had applied himself to thinking about Coleridge's relevance when the issues were residually to live for himself, and he could not dismiss them thereafter. He was the person on the spot to do a job that only he could do, although his feelings concerning the result were as divided as the participants.

Greswell grew up in a landscape that was in process having been discovered earlier by Wordsworth and Coleridge. A hundred years before them, adventurous travellers like Edward Drewe had wandered northwards into the Valley of the Rocks at Lynton, and Richard Warner had found the little church at Culbone;[4] but those who travelled from the east, like Warner, had moved through western Somerset fairly quickly and easily. They had no reason to linger in Stowey until they became aware of what Wordsworth and Coleridge found there. This began to be written about by William Luke Nichols in 1873, who came to stay and, indeed, said more or less everything that needed to be said; and it was quickly abetted by Mrs. Sandford's life of her uncle, Thomas Poole, in 1888. After that time the trickle became a flood and Nichols was not the first: see the colourful Mortimer Collins in 1870 (**48**). Nor was Mrs. Sandford the second: see Alice King (**16**) in 1885 and Arthur Humphreys (**55–57**) in 1885–1889. Nor was any of this the best that could be said: see above in my Chap. 3 on item **49**, whose author I failed to identify. One must nevertheless reckon that during these years, from the early 1870s onwards, while Greswell was assimilating and ordering his Coleridge project, such publications crossed his mind. He wrote "Coleridge and the Quantock Hills" for *Macmillan's Magazine* 56 (1887) 413–20, and this was followed by other essays by him (including essays on Wordsworth) in 1889, 1891, 1893,[5] 1895, and 1896. It led to an awareness celebrated in George Gissing's novel, *The Odd Women* (1893), where Dr. Madden worshipped Tennyson but could never pass Coleridge's cottage "without bowing in spirit."

At a distance, the example of Dove Cottage had raised its head and proved more urgent after Rydal Mount became too expensive to purchase by subscription. In 1890, Stopford Brooke published a pamphlet appealing for donations to purchase the Town End cottage for the general public. Edward Dowden published his unexpectedly bestselling edition of *Lyrical Ballads 1798* during the same year, and the cottage was purchased and opened to the public without delay in July 1891. This was a huge success and worked hand-in-hand with Greswell's repetitious attempts to do something of the same for Coleridge. His "Coleridge and Quantock Hills" (1887) contains at page 416, a paragraph-long description of the cottage and its present sad state as village inn. In 1991, David Miall described how Greswell wrote a letter to the daily *Telegraph* under the

---

[4] For Drewe, see "The Rapt Bard. Written in the Valley of the Stones, near Linton in Devonshire," in *Poems, Chiefly by Gentlemen of Devonshire and Cornwall*. Bath: R. Crutttwell, 1792, 1: 32–36. For Warner, see *A Walk through some of the Western Counties of England*. Bath: R. Cruttwell, 1800, pp. 93–103.

[5] In *The Westminster Budget* 23 June 1893, 34. I mention this journal-title because it was one less used by Greswell.

pseudonym, "Wayfarer," on 9 September 1892, which led to a discussion both local and national through the following months involving Edmund Gosse as a most prominent naysayer, and Greswell was at hand for the placement of a memorial plaque a year later. He was the obvious person to serve as a secretary to save the cottage, to deal with the sticky problems arising from local lack of interest—even opposition—while William Knight and Ernest Harley Coleridge involved themselves in national fundraising activities. He extended his claims on Coleridge's behalf to an improbably exaggerated extent in "The Witchery of the Quantock Hills" *Temple Bar* 104 (1895): 523–36, where he argued for the influence on Coleridge of Andrew Crosse.[6] He wrote in more measured terms in *The Athenæum* (No. 3570, 18 March 1896: 413) on the need for money to make the cottage a local Coleridge library: his lifelong ideal. The project advanced unsteadily towards a half-successful conclusion late in 1907 and was handed over to the nation in 1908. The Stowey cottage as a simple visitor attraction has never been such a popular venue, like Dove Cottage, though its fortunes have risen a little during recent years.

Greswell guardedly involved himself with preservation, but Wordsworth is quoted more often than Coleridge in his writing; indeed, Wordsworth was oddly closer to Greswell's way of thinking. One wonders if Greswell was in two minds about his support: saw the way things would turn out with a degree of reluctance. The cottage might have been for him, as it was for Mark Rutherford—remembered as "small, somewhat squalid rooms. Pity, pity, almost to tears"—a place to get away from, if only into the garden and thence into the wider countryside that, like Coleridge, Greswell so loved to escape into. But it was an obligation he fully recognized while he did not widely advertise his duties. He acted as the local agent and efficient circulator of material, while Coleridge's grandson and Professor Knight proselytized at the front of the house. Coleridge gets only a passing mention in two of his later books, and in his final years, when the Cottage proved unsuccessful, he thought more about rescuing Aldenham House as a local library.

---

[6] An amateur scientist and experimenter in electricity, who was born and died at Fyne Court at Broomfied. Born 1784, died 1855, he was fourteen years old in 1798.

CHAPTER 8

A Brave Conclusion

Abstract Greswell's venture was odd in its time, and avoids the Oxford trio of Arnold, Jowett and Green. But looking again at his arrangement, one might discern the recognition of the challenge that Carlyle's critique represents in the first half of the sequence, and perhaps the recognition of a solution embedded if not followed through in the second half. Carlyle's "Natural Supernaturalism" became the fashionable norm a century later in Meyer Abrams' restatement of it, and Seeley's "Natural Religion" became, despite his protests, the common denominator in humanistic deism. Martineau's 1856 essay (no. **29**) fits in because it was written at the beginning of a moment of change that was completed during the period Greswell's book was put together. It followed two years after Martineau's struggle with Chapman over the Utilitarian direction not taken by the *Westminster Review*, at a time when Martineau was engaged with Sidgwick over fundamental differences that culminated in, respectively, Sidgwick's *The Methods of Ethics* (1874 etc.) and his own *Types of Ethical Theory* (1885 etc.). And perhaps Greswell positioned Martineau's essay in the pivotal place it occupies for this very reason. It places Coleridge at a moment of change. It makes a case for Coleridge's significance, against Carlyle's crude misrepresentation, at the very moment when that significance was being challenged by other, stronger voices.

Martineau began with conscience: the intersection of philosophy, theology and psychology; the peculiar mix—not balance—between Utilitarianism and Christianity. Pater refused the polite alternative, and

---

© The Author(s), under exclusive license to Springer Nature Switzerland AG 2023
J. C. C. Mays, *Coleridge in William Greswell's Workbook*, https://doi.org/10.1007/978-3-031-38593-3_8

95

thereby avoided the obfuscation that Arnold's Oxford manner carries on its boots like invisible mud. The Oxford circles represented by Greswell's uncles might have engaged, if only to a qualified extent, with the adversarial stance represented by Arnold's "culture" but Pater, following in his essay where Allsop left off (no. **36**), is a direct challenge concerning what Coleridge's legacy is really about. Pater's statement, even though it is a more open, less class-conscious argument for the importance of culture than Greswell would have wanted, points in the new direction that attracted him. Finally, Mozley earns his place for the sheer bravado of maintaining a truth he could not substantiate (no.**45**). George Craik had earlier made a similar enthusiastic case for Coleridge's later poetry, but it was lost in a storm. What more to say than that Greswell's book adventitiously points to the deep, true line in Coleridge criticism.

Keywords Summing-up • Greswell's book was odd in its time because it describes an old argument which has rumbled on through the twentieth century and still holds the majority opinion • How his attention to Martineau, Pater and Mozley points in a different direction: a more positive and exciting realisation of Coleridge's greatness

1 Returning to Sum-Up

William Greswell was born into a family steeped in theological discussion, unafraid to take positions on the conservative side of debates that divided intellectual life. He did not publicly rebel but as a young man, he certainly appears to have explored his options. He avoided Balliol, where his father had been a tutor before Jowett and T. H. Green showed a way out of belief. Like many of his generation, he was in search of a less dogmatic and more ahistorical stance, but not at the cost of losing his faith. He found himself at a moment when recent intellectual history appeared to be repeating itself: the same again, but more dramatically (creation of the earth, evolution of species, disintegration of the book of truth); and he kept any involvement that he had in such problems to himself and left no evidence that he proselytized directly on behalf of any cause. In later life, he expressed opinions on a large number of topics—politics, economics, the formation of civil society, historical figures—but he never recurred to the issues raised by the discussion of Coleridge. One must suppose that he later valued Coleridge for less than half a dozen poems centred on a feeling for place, and was only glad to mention Coleridge's brief residence when he came to write books of local history.

His collection of Coleridgean writings represents a crisis of conscience not as loud or decisive as that of the younger Froude, nor as assimilated as in Mrs. Humphry Ward's *Robert Elsmere*. If crisis is the word, it was presented at a remove from the person facing it: not focused on a mirroring counterpart, but in the disagreements surrounding counterparts who had become historical figures. The construction of the collection suggests how this was understood and how it was left behind. The separate contributions at first appear parcelled-up as if they were being tidied, as remnants and souvenirs. The sense of detachment might be due to them having been in part supplied by a contemporary who shared Greswell's sense of spiritual uncertainty, but the sense of individual response is no less distinctive. It is far less decisive than, for example, the straight line of descent that Boodle was able to draw upon to deliver his own minor place in history. For Greswell, one might say Coleridge stood for a series of contradictory ideas and values that do not mix but are vital, along with a couple of poems that continued to celebrate the spirit of the place in which he was born and died.

The position Greswell occupied is not unique. People as different as Arnold ("What he himself meant by the buried self is never quite clear": Robbins. 165), William Hale White, and Seeley found themselves in a *fin-de-siècle* cul-de-sac that became habitual. The intellectual wars over belief throughout the 1830s, 1840s and 1850s had been loud, angry and—in the long term—inconclusive. When they appeared to advance towards a climax in *Essays and Reviews* (1860), it was—despite but also because of their consequences—a climax that delivered an apparent victory for the conservative side that at the same time allowed the other, radical, side space to gain a more secure acceptance. Again, *Robert Elsmere* shows what was won and lost in the interval, and it appears Greswell did not approve.

I return to Greswell's unusual focus on Coleridge and emphasize that it was an odd venture at the time. No one—including James Dykes Campbell and Ernest Hartley Coleridge, who both assembled copies of Coleridge texts—chased down such a wide-ranging collection of other persons' views. Coleridge's name was not one to conjure with in a primarily theological context as it had been in the 1830s and 1840s. And meantime, and especially if one was looking back over the intervening decades, what Coleridge stood for had become muddled with his prominent and varying spokespersons' ideas: that is, with the Broad Church Movement and Christian Socialism. Greswell chose a way of looking that takes pains to avoid such a close link with the deeper past. He also steps outside the most obvious signifying presences that hovered over the Oxford of his generation: I mean—in the 1870s and 1880s—Clough and Arnold, Jowett and Green. Pater's first important publication is significant, and it points in the new, aesthetic direction that criticism was moving towards. Looking again at Greswell's arrangement, one might discern the recognition of the challenge that Carlyle's critique represents in the first half of the sequence, and perhaps the recognition of a solution working out in the second half of the same. The problem meanwhile remains: one is left uncertain how conscious Greswell is of such conjunctions, or (here) how seriously they should be taken. Coleridge again became a name to conjure with in the verse and criticism of the 1880s and 1890s, but for quite different reasons than those that interested Greswell.

To repeat, Greswell was caught between his older family and younger friends. He grasped at Coleridge's Unitarian beginnings, and American Transcendentalism found an important place in his library, and this led him to the same dead end as several other roads he might have taken. But he came to be able to put the impasse behind him and live a life, pondering the traces of other lives in the place he had grown up in. When he referred to Tulloch's essay in the *Fortnightly Review* (January 1885—item **32**) in his late list of library holdings, he had obviously forgotten that it once held a significant place in his argument against Traill. I think now we are pretty much in the same place as we were in the 1880s with respect to the spiritual crisis involved. It has only become different in having become more securely embedded. It is the new norm, no longer a crisis but a condition, and it now sits alongside modes of belief and behaviour one would have thought incompatible a hundred and more years ago. We live together as best we can, and the need to know what Coleridge thought is not obviously pressing.

2   A SECOND TAKE

The interval between when Greswell graduated and took orders was a period in which he "took time out" to think about what he was doing with his life. We don't know, when he went to South Africa, if he had more in mind: that is, if he was already interested in the "South Africa problem" and wanted to learn more about it. Or if he discovered the problems of

South Africa once he was there, that he wanted to write about them, that he discovered he could first make a living by sorting them out.

To return again to Greswell's state of mind during and following his undistinguished Oxford BA: the four brothers, father and uncles who were alive throughout this period, died towards its close and afterwards. Edward, at Corpus, died in 1869; his father William, formerly at Balliol, died in 1876; Richard, at Worcester, died in 1881; and Clement, formerly at Oriel, died in 1882. The big battles over geology, evolution and the Higher Criticism had come to a head in *Essays and Reviews*. This was followed by Roman Catholic conversion, and atheism, but for the larger part was marked by a drift towards a more "natural" religion from all directions. Some of Greswell's Oxford contemporaries (Boodle and Holmes) were very clear about how they saw the way forward. Greswell was not; possibly because of his background, in which he saw much with which he did not agree but also saw more that was already part of his nature and which he did not want to reject. For example, his uncle Richard at Worcester College worked extraordinarily hard and generously on behalf of social and educational causes. And I might also repeat that, although Seeley's religious position in *Ecce Homo* and *Natural Religion* was taken by many at the time as an expression of a religious position based upon morality rather than anything supernatural, he himself protested against such assumptions. Religious beliefs are usually more complicated than the formulations they receive and, while Greswell's book shows up the contradictions involved in Coleridge's reputation, it would appear that complete consistency in such matters is unlikely to be achieved.

Greswell left no record of such thoughts, unless it is contained in his book of reviews. If the accumulation bore on his thinking, the way he chose to arrange it, ten or fifteen years later, is curiously detached. The lasting impression given is of nuggets of truth among a heap of repetitive positions. One could reckon that, by the time he was installed in Dodington Rectory, the Coleridge venture was an event in the past that was preserved—bound up "for the record"—and forgotten.

I have remarked before that Greswell's prose style is noteworthy for his fluent and vivid descriptions. See his South Africa-book description of 1820 settlers landing at what became Port Elizabeth (1: 81–86), or his "Early Summer at the Cape" in *Murray's Magazine* 7 (1890): 818–28). His feeling for landscape is easily communicated, ideas and people less so, in so far as they are attempted at all. What does this say about his ability to handle ideas in general? He picks them up in the separate essays/reviews but usually sets them down in a way that makes, in effect, a withdrawal to a further distance. So particular issues are acknowledged but no real decision taken. A bystander's view is maintained and a passive acceptance of the status quo, despite the objections, remains; or, more generously, an instinctive faith in a traditional stance.

One might compare what Wilfred Stone says about William Hale White: his lack of interest in Coleridge's ideas and, instead, his love of the beauty in natural forms and colours, as if he found in them certain restorative powers (Wilfred Stone, 70). The simple emotional response to nature is similarly easy in Greswell's writing; tender delicacy, passionate restraint, a real love, the descriptive impulse springing from it. He sees at best as if by an inner light that makes things glow. There are cascading, intoxicating lists of plant names, like Ralph Cusack's in the much later novel *Cadenza* (1958), Cusack being the only literary author to have a plant catalogue reviewed for its style in the *TLS*. And did Greswell share some of White's timidity? Holding back? There is no reason to think he thought much more of Coleridge's cottage than Edward Thomas did: a dull place at the exit of a village which explains why Coleridge spent so much time outdoors.

Despite his incorporation of Mozley's argument, Greswell finds more in Wordsworth. See the effective quotation of the sonnet—"We must be free or die, who speak the tongue | Which Shakespeare spake"—which closes the opening chapter of *South Africa* (1: 36). Wordsworth's lines strike notes that Coleridge never attempted, despite the several opportunities in poems he wrote during the period 1796–1803. Greswell's sojourn abroad—short and possibly interrupted as it might have been—brought forward the underlying conservatism in his nature. One might again recall Boodle, for whom the longer time away, in a place that appeared to have a brighter future, brought greater clarity of mind. He was the more probing and incisive, more accomplished in articulating problematic ideas, and explicit in defining his own position. He accumulated thirty-six large volumes of postcards of Somerset villages, which are now in the Bath Record Office (stored in the basement of the Guildhall): a more tangible record of the place where he was born. Or one might contrast Seeley, in respect both of his historical-political ideas and his theological position. Greswell follows at a distance in this respect, the deliberately more ordinary man.

3   Cui Bono?

The Latin phrase—meaning, to whom is it a benefit?—is most often heard in criminal circumstances, wherein those who profit from a crime find themselves among the first suspects. I intend it here in a literal, more positive sense: meaning for *whose* good? Ad *cuius* bonum? What carries forward from poking about in Greswell's old book? What benefit today? Is Coleridge worth more than a cup of coffee in an over-restored guidebook trap?

I would argue that a careful and informed reading of Greswell's book will support the view that the conventional interpretation of Coleridge's career—in other words, a process towards evaporation—is a distorted version of the truth. Carlyle's "Natural Supernaturalism" and Seeley's "Natural Religion" dominated the mid-twentieth-century understanding of Imagination. John Beer wrote of how it fed into the writing of writers like E. M. Forster and Virginia Woolf, and interprets it as a vague deism. This is handy but inaccurate. It fits, for example, feeling about environmental issues, but it is lazily close to the universal condition that Coleridge called Spinozism. The dissenting aspect of his thinking—especially Unitarianism as it developed away from its crude beginnings—leads to a better understanding of how he contributed to the move out of an intellectual cul-de-sac. From a point of view that sustains Greswell's interest, it is a strain of nineteenth-century thinking that did not run into the sand but sustained a new revival of Coleridge's own poetry from the 1860s. If one holds onto this, it restores the balance between old and new in his achievement and legacy. It maintains a focus on the transcendent alongside the transcendental.

The mix is important. It applies to the Supernatural not as Gothic but as genuine Otherness. It applies to the quality of Coleridge's poetry as well as to the content of his ideas. Perhaps the above will be granted, if only notionally, as an aid to understanding. More difficult—and less likely to be granted—is the Other in personal relationships. It is a mystery, a matter of conscience. It is a position evolved through dialogue with many authorities, not all of them in Coleridge's case on respectable maps. It crosses boundaries: for example, not only between religion and mythology but between philosophy and psychology.

This can be looked at another way, through Coleridge as a moral philosopher and as an influence on Martineau. Or better say that the pair of them reached coincident positions with respect to the goodness and

102   J. C. C. MAYS

badness of moral character: in both cases, they rest their case on a retro-spective assessment of motives. I have mentioned how Martineau's *Ethics* is a long dialogue with Sidgwick, whose emphasis was on the rightness and wrongness of acts performed. Call it a debate on the nature of conscience: religious versus secular. Martineau's advance along the same path as Coleridge—the break with Necessitarianism and the discovery of German philosophy—was easier. Martineau was by nature a more accomplished abstract thinker, but one might think Coleridge's acute personal prob-lems—originating as they did in what he called a sense of absence—made the need for a comforter and saviour the more intense. Intentions (motives) were more important than the act performed, and Wordsworth put the matter well in well-known lines of *The Borderers*:

> The motion of a muscle—this way or that—
> 'Tis done—and in the after vacancy
> We wonder at ourselves like men betrayed:
> Suffering is permanent, obscure and dark,
> And shares the nature of infinity.[1]

Martineau's essay (no. **29**) does not point towards where we find our-selves today. Carlyle's natural supernaturalism became the fashionable norm a century later in Abrams' restatement of it, and Seeley's natural religion became, despite his protests, the common denominator in human-istic deism. The later position enables an easier dialogue in multicultural classrooms, but at the cost of imposing a solution onto a situation it does not fit. I reiterate that, for Coleridge studies, the prevailing situation does not make sense.

Martineau's 1856 essay fits in because it was written at the beginning of a moment of change that was completed during the time Greswell's book was put together, certainly by the time the Coleridge Cottage was incorporated into his legacy. It followed two years after Martineau's strug-gle with Chapman over the Utilitarian direction not taken by the *Westminster Review* (Ashton. Chap. 6), at a time when Martineau was engaged with Sidgwick over fundamental differences that culminated in, respectively, Sidgwick's *The Methods of Ethics* (1874 etc.) and his own *Types of Ethical Theory* (1885 etc.). Martineau's position was close to, if not

---

[1] *The Borderers* (1842), lines 1540–44.

founded on Coleridge or Coleridge's same sources: Sidgwick's was entirely secular, and prevailed to set the parameters of twentieth-century discussion.

The important point is that Martineau's thinking at large, whatever the differences from Coleridge that made him a Unitarian, operates within a horizon that has ceased to be that of the majority and remains so in the present time. And perhaps Greswell positioned Martineau's essay in the pivotal place it occupies for this very reason. It places Coleridge at a moment of change. It makes a case for Coleridge's significance, against Carlyle's crude misrepresentation, at the very moment when that significance was being challenged by other, stronger voices.

The importance of the division between Martineau and Sidgwick cannot be over-emphasised. Their different understanding of act and agency measures the difference between the way goodness and badness is judged: the way individuals suppose they stand in relation to ideals. Martineau, like Coleridge, centres this on a retrospective understanding of motives, of the character of moral agents, and Sidgwick on the rightness and wrongness of acts. The difference may seem straightforward, but it registers a gulf between two worlds. Martineau was interested in the difference between regret and remorse, and Sidgwick in pursuing an active live condition which co-exists alongside a moralistic religious outlook. Coleridge attempted to explain it in his play, *Remorse*: see what he says in a letter to Southey, dated 8 February 1813 (*CL* 3: 433–34), on "the Anguish & Disquietude arising from the Self-contradiction introduced into the Soul by Guilt."

I suggest this difference is paralleled in the different emphases of Coleridge's descriptions of the creative process in Chaps. 13 and 14 of *Biographia Literaria* and in the essays on Method that conclude the 1818 *Friend*. Despite the triumphant and famous statement of *Biographia* Chap. 13, Chap. 14 is clearer about the origins of creativity that fashions unity in variety. Coleridge's own note of dissatisfaction with the Chap. 13 formulation of Imagination is frequently cited (*BL* 1: 304 fn), but Chap. 14 makes the point that, while one struggles to explain what poetry is in terms of its components, one is better advised to ask what the poet is doing. I only pause to note how this turn—from the well-wrought urn to the genie within, from the artefact to the process of its making—disturbed literary theorists of the mid-twentieth century greatly. The essays on Method make the same, central point.

To return to Martineau and Sidgwick on conscience: the topic was central for Coleridge. The ethical ground of self-consciousness is "an experience"—as opposed to a conceptualisation—"of the human will with reason and religion" (*LS* 66). It goes back to the Conclusion of Part I of *Christabel* and before—"Thou'st had thy Will!" (line 306).[2] Coleridge and Martineau were both on the losing side of history; history cannot be rewritten, and there is no question of recovering a situation that has been overtaken. At the same time, there is value in recognising the gulf that exists, to see what is on the other side without obstruction and distortion. The issue becomes clearer in relation to Coleridge's poetry, where a reader is not trying to raise a dead thing but aiming to be involved in a live one. A poem is not a witness to be assessed against others in a historical debate: it already contains the truth if only we can read it. Everyone starts afresh every time they read, and we have neither need nor reason to read verse through the grime it has accumulated: for example, the rubbish heaped on it by Carlyle.

Martineau's agent-based ethics develops alongside Coleridge's idea of conscience but fails to break the Utilitarian link.[3] Coleridge's idea is based on the supposition of creative opposites, the divine conjoined with the human, and has a richer, more complicated psychology. At the same time, Martineau's essay (and, further, his philosophical resistance to Sidgwick's argument on ethics) remains a pointer to what has been lost in the argument. Put another way, I suspect that a reading of Martineau's and Coleridge's views on the authority of the Bible alongside one another would reveal a coincidence of views that would serve to reinforce the authority of both. They would not quite coincide—Coleridge was always looking for the permanent truth buried in dim, poetical sources—but the coincidence might help rescue a deep truth that has been lost.

---

[2] See the sensitive attention to this passage by Theodore Watts-Dunton in his *Poetry and the Renascence of Wonder*. London: Herbert Jenkins, 1916. pp. 272–74.

[3] For a contemporary and strictly philosophical attempt to revive Martineau's ethics, see Michael Slote, *Morals from Motives* (Oxford: Oxford University Press, 2001). Slote locates Martineau's sources in a mainly English and Scottish line that was alien to Coleridge, and the latter was more responsive to German sources and his own self-analysis (often allowed more rein in his poems). For a broader attempt to apply Virtue Ethics to Romantic writers, see Laurence S. Lockridge, "The Coleridge Circle: Virtue Ethics, Sympathy, and Outrage." *Humantitas* (Washington, DC) 29: 1 & 2 (2016), 43–78.

8 A BRAVE CONCLUSION   105

4   UNWRITING HISTORY

One can often insert a figure into a completed history when this does not involve fundamental change, just broadening one's point of view: for example, Thomas Traherne into seventeenth-century literary history and John Clare into the nineteenth. William Blake, who is another intruder, is now no less than Byron part of a jockeying team. One can also insert concepts into history which, on rare occasions, change the actual nature of the history: for example, the position of women or so-called "coloured" writers. This last change is still in process—there is still a proportion of "protest vote" which may not yet have stabilised—but it is no less a fact: it has changed the way we actually think about writing. This is also a reminder of the pernicious Carlyle/Sterling slander at the negative core of Greswell's volume: the prevailing judgement that it set out to overcome. The slander was perhaps justified on the limited evidence available at the time, but it persists. It continued through the twentieth century, underlying attackers (René Wellek persistently, Norman Fruman more circuitously), and even otherwise generous defenders (see, e.g. Richard Holmes's sad second volume of Coleridge biography, *Darker Reflections* 1998). It continues today—see the arguments about Coleridge's abandonment of radical politics, or the treatment of his wife and family, or his turn to a difficult philosophy—but why? It was the primary aim and achievement of the Bollingen Coleridge to explode the myth, but it did not succeed?[4] The three heroes of the later part of Greswell's sequence point the necessary way.

Martineau began with conscience: the intersection of philosophy, theology and psychology; the peculiar mix—not balance—between Utilitarianism and Christianity. Pater refused the polite alternative, and thereby avoided the obfuscation that Arnold's Oxford manner carries on its boots like invisible mud. The Oxford circles represented by Greswell's uncles might have engaged, if only to a qualified extent, with the adversarial stance represented by Arnold's "culture" but Pater, following in his essay where Allsop left off, is a direct challenge concerning what Coleridge's legacy is really about. Pater's statement, even though it is a more open, less class-conscious argument for the importance of culture than Greswell would have wanted to support, points in the new direction that attracted

---

[4]See my *Coleridge's Dejection Ode* (New York: Palgrave Macmillan, 2019), Chap. 2, on this persistent aberration of public taste.

him. Finally, Mozley earns his place for the sheer bravado of maintaining a truth he could not substantiate. George Craik had already made an enthusiastic case for Coleridge's later poetry, beyond the few poems on which his popular reputation was based, but whatever he had to say was drowned out by voices that repeated what others wanted to hear as they trundled through the platitudes. Craik even, like Mozley, devoted a paragraph to describing why "Love, Hope, and Patience in Education" was "the happiest and most perfect" of all Coleridge's poems.[5]

Mozley's argument rested on Coleridge's alternative way as a poet outside any ambition to gain fame as one, and as a philosopher free to use poetry to do things that philosophy could not do alone. His general argument is cogent but it fails to persuade because it lacks detail. It does not attempt to show how the "sweet new style" Coleridge developed in "Dejection: an Ode" carries forward into a sequence of tableaux in which allegorical figures like Love and Hope constantly re-group on a silent stage. Patience joins the mix here, with wasted overtones of suffering and even of Christ's Passion. In "The Improvisatore," she is "Contentment"; in "Duty, Surviving Self-love," she is "a blank Lot"; in "The Pang More Sharp than All," it is "Kindness counterfeiting absent Love!" As Mozley says, Coleridge's independence of mind led to a poetry of greater subtlety and scope than any of his contemporaries, and continued to develop up to the day of his death. Mozley does not waste time on the reasons why its qualities have been overlooked, but it is not enough to supply only its intellectual credentials. One has to show how such poetry is read by an audience that has been deafened by noise, blinded by artificial light and consumed by consumables.

Greswell's trio of pointers beyond the main bulk of his collection; I think to its most valuable component. They don't quite say anything he said himself, but they aim to embrace positions that (a) appear to be irreconcilable (Martineau), (b) despite the discomfort and affront that might involve (Pater), and (c) with a consciousness of not taking anything for granted (Mozley). A refurbished cottage that satisfies curiosity and offers a welcome break from heavy driving is not good enough; in fact, it is pathetic. Greswell somehow appears to have realized this, and the three remarkable, anomalous essays he positioned in the second half of his survey register an interpretation that still needs to be better heard.

---

[5] I have gone over this poem yet again in *The Coleridge Bulletin* NS 59 (Summer 2022), 29–38, trying to explain its intricacies.

SELECTED GRESWELL BIBLIOGRAPHY[1]

Aherne, Philip. "The 'way of seeking': The Coleridgean Development of Utilitarianism in Cambridge." In *Coleridge and Contemplation*. Ed. Peter Cheyne. Oxford: Oxford UP, 2017. 104–22.
An essay important in the present context because it gathers evidence to which scholarship has been relatively blind until recently; namely, how Coleridge's influence extended beyond the middle years of the nineteenth century and F. D. Maurice. In the context of Greswell's collection, it applies to the important position occupied by Mozley's essay (item **45**) and John Seeley (both not included by Aherne).
———. *The Coleridge Legacy: Samuel Taylor Coleridge's Intellectual Legacy in Britain and America, 1834–1934*. London: Palgrave Macmillan, 2018.
Important not least because of the conjoining of Coleridge's legacy from both sides of the Atlantic. Greswell, and whoever helped gather his Coleridge materials, showed what could be learned from such an exercise a 150 years earlier, and does not slight the short-lived new impetus towards the end of the nineteenth century.
Altholz, Josef L. *The Religious Press in Britain, 1760–1900*. New York: Greenwood, 1989. Contributions to the Study of Religion, 22.

---

[1] The items that comprise the text of Greswell's book, listed **1–60** in Chap. 4, are not included (with the exception under Mozley of item **45**). The annotations in blue following many items contain comments on their relevance, when this is not obvious. They might be read, in lieu of thickets of footnotes, as a Latin *recursus*: a reminder of the journey travelled.

© The Author(s), under exclusive license to Springer Nature Switzerland AG 2023
J. C. C. Mays, *Coleridge in William Greswell's Workbook*, https://doi.org/10.1007/978-3-031-38593-3

107

108 SELECTED GRESWELL BIBLIOGRAPHY

Ashton, Rosemary. "Doubting Clerics: From James Anthony Froude to *Robert Elsmere* via George Eliot." In *The Critical Spirit and the Will to Believe: Essays in Nineteenth-Century Literature and Religion*. Ed. David Jasper and T. R. Wright. New York: St. Martin's Press, 1989. 69–87.

See on Froude and Mrs. Humphry Ward below.

———. *142 Strand: A Radical Address in Victorian London*. London: Chatto and Windus, 2006.

Centred on the campaigning publisher, John Chapman, who edited the *Westminster Review* from 1852 and introduced a generation of Oxford-educated young men to others involved in unorthodox ("infidel") causes.

Beer, John. "Coleridge's Elusive Presence among the Victorians." In his *Romantic Influences: Contemporary—Victorian—Modern*. Basingstoke, Hants.: The Macmillan Press, 1993. 147–68 (Chap. 6).

A demonstration of how Coleridge's later nineteenth-century reputation as a thinker was shaped by false judgements—in particular by Carlyle in his *Life of Sterling*—that took hold during his lifetime. A selection of the material is repeated, alongside other details, in Beer's introduction to the Bollingen edition of *Aids to Reflection* (1993). cxxxiii–cxlix.

Bell, Duncan. *The Idea of Greater Britain: Empire and the Future of World Order, 1860–1900*. Princeton: Princeton UP, 2007.

The book builds on earlier essays by Bell published in scholarly journals, several of which cited Greswell in relation to Seeley. Seeley emerges as the most articulate spokesperson of the federal idea before it was overtaken by imperialism (see e.g. pp. 108–130) and Chap. 6 is dedicated to Seeley and the theological inflexion of his vision of a greater Britain.

———. *Reordering the World: Essays on Liberalism and Empire*. Princeton: Princeton UP, 2016.

Chapter 11 is another essay on Seeley and "the Political Theology of Empire" in the context of thinkers such as John Stuart Mill, Sidgwick and E. A. Freeman. Greswell continues to be cited as "formerly a Professor of Classics in South Africa" (p. 144).

Boodle, Richard William. "Modern Pessimism" *Canadian Monthly* 3 (June 1879): 591–601.

Boodle's contributions to the Toronto journal—a selection of which are listed here and below—were published under the editorship of George Mercer Adam, with the co-operation of Goldwin Smith and others.

———. "The Arthur of History and Romance." *Canadian Monthly* 5 (December 1880): 582–88.

———. "Mr. Mallock: A Retrospect" *Canadian Monthly* 6 (Feb 1881): 195–203. See below under Mallock.

———. "Mr Mallock's 'Romance of the 19th Century': A Review" *Canadian Monthly* 7 (September 1881): 322–27.

SELECTED GRESWELL BIBLIOGRAPHY 109

———. "Natural Religion 1" *Popular Science Monthly* 22 (Feb 1883): 511–21. Online at <https://en.wikisource.org/wiki/Popular_Science_Monthly>, accessed 17 February 2019.

The journal was founded in 1872 by two brothers Edward and William Youmans and published by D. Appleton and Company. It quickly became an outlet for new ideas (Darwin, Huxley, etc.), and it published four instalments of what became Seeley's book (*Natural Religion*, 1882), between May and December 1875, under the title "The Deeper Harmonies of Science and Religion: 1–4." In other words, Boodle's two-part review was part of a campaign in which the publishers were heavily invested (see Ungureanu below). Each part is subtitled "A STUDY IN THE GROWTH OF SCIENTIFIC MORALITY."

Boodle's discussion proceeds by way of reviewing the religious history of the previous thirty years. He writes of "the hollowness of Coleridge's religious compromises" on the first page (p. 511); describes 1873 and 1874 as "years of open utterance on all sides," "the crisis of the revolution of thought" (p. 515), and cites the close of Pater's *Studies in the History of the Renaissance* among other texts (p. 515), claiming that this has left behind a short period of pessimism and despair together with the sense of a need for reconstruction. It amounts, in effect, to a narrative of the intellectual-spiritual happenings during the years Greswell and Boodle grew up, which built to a crisis during their time at Oxford.

———. "Natural Religion 2" *Popular Science Monthly* 22 (March 1883): 606–15. Online at <https://en.wikisource.org/wiki/Popular_Science_Monthly>, accessed 17 February 2019.

The focus moves to the 1882 publication, arguing that "the writer is clearly himself a believer in supernaturalism, if not as very tangible, yet as an underlying possibility" (p. 606): "the minimum basis of a faith without a personal God and without miracles, is a compromise honestly offered by one who himself apparently still cherishes these beliefs" (p. 607). The discussion ends with quotations from Leslie Stephen and Aristotle, and an acknowledgement of the persistence of the supernatural, the unknowable in an age of science, as a kind of aspirant humanism: "as far as possible to think the thoughts of immortals, and to live in our every act up to the noblest part within us" (closing words on p. 615).

Brady, Ciaran. *James Anthony Froude: An Intellectual Biography of a Victorian Prophet*. Oxford: Oxford UP, 2013.

Bruce, Robert V. *Bell: Alexander Graham Bell and the Conquest of Solitude*. London: Victor Gollancz, 1973.

Bell taught at Somersetshire College for a year (Sept 1866–July 1867), immediately following Greswell's departure. The school at that time had about a hundred pupils, a high staff-student ratio and an adventurous hiring policy (pp. 52–53).

110 SELECTED GRESWELL BIBLIOGRAPHY

Buell, Lawrence. *Literary Transcendentalism: Style and Vision in the American Renaissance*. Ithaca, NY: Cornell UP, 1973.

Burgon, John William. *Lives of Twelve Good Men*. 2 vols. London: John Murray, 1888. Vol. 2: 93–121—the seventh essay in the volume—is devoted to "Richard Greswell: The Faithful Steward." It is very largely based on the accounts of others, collected by a younger graduate of the same Oxford college. Richard is described as a modest and retiring Oxford don, with strongly held conventional opinions. He published little (unlike his brother Edward, at Corpus) but was most generous in employing the money he did not need on good causes—especially to further the cause of National Christian Education. He took a special interest in Central Africa and the putting down of the slave trade and, though failing in health in his later years, must have been a difficult presence for his undergraduate nephew at BNC to ignore.

Call, Wathen Mark Wilks. *Reverberations. Second Edition, to which is prefixed The Growth of Opinion which Made Me Leave the Church*. London: Trübner, 1876. The autobiographical essay was retitled "A Chapter from my Autobiography" on pp. 3–38 and used to introduce the posthumous volume *Final Causes: a Refutation* (London: Kegan Paul, 1891).
Call was the author/editor of items **2–3**. His conversion by, and subsequent disenchantment with, Coleridge's ideas would have reminded contemporaries of John Sterling, especially as commemorated in Carlyle's *Life* (1851).

Campbell, James Dykes (ed.). *The Poetical Works of Samuel Taylor Coleridge*. London: Macmillan, 1893.
Identifies Wathen Call as the author/editor of the Coleridge letters published in *Westminster Review* 1870 (items **2** and **3**) on page xcv note.

———. *Samuel Taylor Coleridge: A Narrative of the Events of his Life. With a Memoir of the Author by Leslie Stephen*. London: Macmillan, 1896.
Identifies Wathen Call as the author/editor of the Coleridge letters published in *Westminster Review* 1870 (items **2** and **3**) on page 212 note.

Carlyle, Thomas. *The Life of Sterling* [1851]. Ed. with an Introduction by W. Hale White. London: Henry Frowde, Oxford UP, 1907. The World's Classics, 144.
Chapter 8 opens with the famous picture of Coleridge on Highgate Hill looking down on London as "a kind of Magus, girt in mystery and enigma," and develops into a description of genius addled by weakness, even dangerous self-deception. The toxic mixture as described by Carlyle gave a new perspective on Coleridge's significance during the second half of the nineteenth century and it helped shape Greswell's views.

Carpenter, J. Estlin. *James Martineau, Theologian and Teacher: A Study of his Life and Thought*. London: Philip Green, 1905. A second issue with index was published later the same year in 615 pages.
As many have since remarked, Carpenter's book laid a heavy stone on Martineau's reputation.

SELECTED GRESWELL BIBLIOGRAPHY   111

Casement, Ann, and David Tacy. *The Idea of the Numinous: Contemporary Jungian and Psychoanalytic Perspectives*. London: Routledge, 2006.

Cockshut, A. O. J. (ed.). *Religious Controversies of the Nineteenth Century: Selected Documents*. London: Methuen, 1966.

A conventional mid-twentieth century anthology of the central texts to set against Greswell's.

Coleridge, Ernest Hartley (ed.). *Letters of Samuel Taylor Coleridge*. 2 vols. London: William Heinemann, 1895.

Of interest for what it deliberately excluded (e.g. the larger context of items 2–3), as well as for all it contrived to include. See also below, under Walters (1971).

Conway, Moncure Daniel. "Religion and Progress: Interpreted by the Life and Last Work of Wathen Mark Wilks Call." *The Monist* (La Salle, IL) 2 (1892): 183–197.

An obituary that celebrates the author's long friendship with the disillusioned Coleridgean and subsequent freethinker who submitted the *Westminster* "Unpublished Letters" in 1870 (items 2–3).

———. *Autobiography: Memories and Experiences*. 2 vols. London: Cassell, 1904.

An American minister (1832–1907), who was in turn a Methodist, a Unitarian and finally a freethinker. He moved to London in 1863, where he remained for a decade or so. His book provides further details on Wathen Call and other members of the Brabant circle (Strauss, George Eliot, etc.).

Cook, Simon J. *The Intellectual Foundations of Alfred Marshall's Economic Science: A Rounded Globe of Knowledge*. Cambridge: Cambridge UP, 2009.

[Courtney, Janet E.] *The Making of an Editor: W. L. Courtney, 1850–1928*. London: Macmillan, 1930.

Courtney, W. L. *Studies at Leisure*. London: Chapman and Hall, 1892.

A collection of essays that displays Courtney's wide interests and intellectual ability. The concluding essay on Martineau, given Greswell's interest, is a measure of the respect in which he was held by non-Unitarians.

———. *The Passing Hour*. London: Hutchinson[, 1925].

Chapters III and VIII on being a pupil at Somersetshire College, Bath, two years behind Greswell, and who was headmaster for a brief period (1873–1876). Editor of *Fortnightly Review*, 1894–1928, following, after an interval, Thomas Hay Sweet Escott—for whom, see below.

Cox, Leo, and J. Harry Smith. *Fifty Years of Brush and Pen: A Historical Sketch of the Pen and Pencil Club of Montreal*. Montreal: Pen and Pencil Club, 1959.

A society, founded by Richard Boodle and five others in March 1890, to promote the arts and literature in Montreal. The substantial records of meetings and contributions by members are preserved in the Musée McCord in Montreal: online at <collections.musee-mccord.qc.ca>, accessed 25 May 2019.

112   SELECTED GRESWELL BIBLIOGRAPHY

[Craik, George L.] Review of S. T. Coleridge *Poetical Works* (3 vols. London: William Pickering, 1834). In *The Printing Machine: or, Companion to the Library* 12 (16 August 1834): 275–79. Reprinted variatim in Craik's *Sketches of the History of Literature and Learning in England: with Specimens of the Principal Writers.* Volume 6. London: Charles Knight, 1845. 139–60.

Craik's review, although naive in tone, is one of the freshest and most interesting that Coleridge's posthumous volumes received. It bravely deplores some of the crudities of the early verse and makes an original case for the poetry that lies beyond that made Coleridge popular in his time. *The Printing Machine*, also published by Charles Knight, was absorbed into Leigh Hunt's *London Journal* in 1835. Craik (1798–1866) wrote for the Society for the Diffusion of Useful Knowledge and, in 1849, became Professor of English Literature and History at Belfast.

Crawford, Walter and Edward S. Lauterbach, with the assistance of Ann M. Crawford. *Samuel Taylor Coleridge: An Annotated Bibliography of Criticism and Scholarship. Volume II: 1900–1939, with additional entries for 1795–1899.* Boston, MA: G. K. Hall, 1983. See also Richard D. Haven.

———, with the research and editorial assistance of Ann M. Crawford. *Samuel Taylor Coleridge: An Annotated Bibliography of Criticism and Scholarship. Volume III: Part 1, 1793–1794 (Supplement to Vols. 1 and II, 1793–1939; Comprehensive Bibliography, 1940–1965; Selective Bibliography, 1966–1994). Part II, 1791–1993.* New York: G. K. Hall, 1996. See also Richard D. Haven.

Davie, Donald. *A Gathered Church: The Literature of the English Dissenting Interests, 1700–1930. The Clark Lectures 1976.* London: Routledge and Kegan Paul, 1978. Reprinted in his *Essays in Dissent: Church, Chapel, and the Unitarian Conspiracy.* Manchester: Carcanet, 1995. 1–111.

A lively argument that attempts to remove Unitarianism from the history of Dissent, supposing the movement a branch of rationalism "with whatever that may imply of imaginative constrictedness and timidity" (68).

DeLaura, David J. "'Coleridge' and the Higher Morality" in his *Hebrew and Hellene in Victorian England: Newman, Arnold, and Pater.* Austin, TX: University of Texas Press, 1969. 192–201 (Chapter 13).

Reads Pater's original 1866 essay on Coleridge as the moment when Newman appeared old hat, Arnold supercilious, and Pater genuinely *au courant*. Pater's essay is interpreted to map out the implications of Arnold's view of religion and culture in a way Arnold never dared to suggest.

Dowden, Edward (ed.). *Lyrical Ballads: Reprinted from the First Edition of 1798.* London: David Nutt, 1890.

Five hundred copies were printed in half-vellum boards at 7/6d, and fifty on large paper. Further editions were published by Nutt in 1891 (1000 copies) and 1898.

SELECTED GRESWELL BIBLIOGRAPHY   113

Drummond, James, and C. B. Upton. *The Life and Letters of James Martineau*. 2 vols. London: James Nisbet, 1902.

Duffy, John J. (ed.). *Coleridge's American Disciples: The Selected Correspondence of James Marsh*. Amherst, MA: The University of Massachusetts Press, 1973.

Ellis, Ieuan. *Seven Against Christ: A Study of "Essays and Reviews."* Leiden: E. J. Brill, 1980. Studies in the History of Christian Thought, 23.

England, Richard. "Censoring Huxley and Wilberforce: A New Source for the Meeting that the *Athenaeum* 'Wisely Softened Down'." *Notes and Records [of the Royal Society London]*. https://doi.org/10.1098/rsnr.2016.0058. Online at <http://rsnr.royalsocietypublishing.org/> accessed 8 November 2018. Describes how uncle Richard Greswell was the first to rise from his seat to oppose the Darwinian theory of evolution in the famous Oxford exchange between William Wilberforce and Thomas Huxley in July 1860. (Other accounts—e.g. Leonard Huxley *The Life and Letters of Thomas Henry Huxley*—London: Macmillan, 1900, I: 202—give Richard Greswell as the second speaker, following Professor Farrar.)

Escott, T[homas] H[ay] S[weet]]. *Platform, Press, Politics and Play; being Pen and Ink Sketches of Contemporary Celebrities from the Tone to the Thames, via Avon and Isis*. Bristol: J. W. Arrowsmith[, 1895]. Escott took private pupils at Oxford following his Second Class BA (Queen's College), 1865–1868; then became lecturer at King's College London and editor of *Fortnightly Review*, 1882–1886 (retired due to illness). See Lysiak below. Bath and its schools occupy Chaps. V–VIII. Chap. VI comments on Escott's father, who was headmaster of Somersetshire College Bath (1858?–1873), where W. L. Courtney succeeded him as headmaster for a brief period (1873–1876) and on Greswell and his father at Kilve.

Festing, Gabrielle. *John Hookham Frere and his Friends*. London: John Nisbet, 1899.

Flitton, Marilyn G. *The Canadian Monthly, 1872–1882*. MA dissertation (TS) submitted Simon Fraser University, April 1973. Online at <https://core.ac.uk/download/pdf/56367024.pdf>, accessed 22 March 2019. Lists Boodle's nine contributions (essays, reviews and verse). *The Canadian Monthly* was modelled on the *Fortnightly Review*, whose stated policy under John Morley—"standard bearer of rationalism against orthodoxy" (Walter Graham *English Literary Periodicals* pp. 259, 260)—was impartiality.

Frere, W. E. and Bartle (eds.). *The Works of John Hookham Frere in Verse and Prose*. 2 vols. London: Basil Montagu Pickering, 1872. NB the 2nd corrected and enlarged ed.—pub 1874—available online at Hathi. The introductory "Memoir," composed primarily by Bartle Frere, extends over pp ix-ccxcv (viz. 286 pages). There are many scattered references to Coleridge, but the full extent of the relationship was not fully evident until the latter's letters were published by Gabrielle Festing *John Hookham Frere and his Friends* (James Nisbet, 1899). 217–29.

114   SELECTED GRESWELL BIBLIOGRAPHY

Froude, James Anthony. *The Nemesis of Faith* (1849), 2nd ed. with an Introduction by William G. Hutchinson. London: The Walter Scott Publishing Co., 1904. Froude was an undergraduate at Oriel at the time when Greswell's uncle Clement was a fellow, and already familiar with the ideas of the Oxford Movement through his elder brother, Hurrell, who died during the year James went up (1836). Froude was ordained deacon in 1845 but soon after began to advertise his religious doubts. The novel (not pseudonymous, like his first) caused clamorous protest, was publicly burned, and compelled him to resign his fellowship at Exeter College.

————. *Oceana: or England and her Colonies.* London: Longmans, Green, 1886. Froude's second visit to the Cape Colony described in *Oceana* took place in 1884–1885; that is, after the trip that frustrated the success of Sir Bartle Frere, to whom Greswell dedicated his own account of Cape history. Frere's South African hero was Sir George Grey, and his position in relation to native Africans and the Dutch was much more aligned with modern thinking. Froude's side of the earlier interventions was published in journal essays and two lectures between 1877 and 1880 (see Brady 479).

Gardiner, John. *Bishops 150: A History of the Diocesan College, Rondebosch. Cape Town:* Juta, 1997. Contains two references to Greswell: (A) Officiating at the first College Sports in June 1879 (p. 168); and (B) as teaching at the College from 1879 to 1883 and being a good cricketer (p. 263).

Gibbins, John Richard. *John Grote: Cambridge University and the Development of Victorian Thought.* Exeter: Imprint Academic, 2007. Describes Mozley as a member of the Grote Society and his interaction with other members such as Alfred Marshall.

Goring, Jeremy. *Martineau, Maurice and the Unitarian Dilemma.* London: Unitarians Publications, 1987. The Essex Hall Lecture, 1987. Online at <http://www.unitarian.org.uk/sites/default/files/1987_Essex_Hall_Lecture.pdf>, accessed 2 July 2019. Maurice, the most-often commented upon conduit of Coleridge's theological ideas through the nineteenth century; Martineau, less often mentioned, but with a mind that tangled with those same ideas at a more interesting level.

Greswell, William Henry Parr. *Our South African Empire.* 2 vols. London: Chapman and Hall, 1885 (All the book-length titles by Greswell listed below are available online through the Hathi Trust Digital Library). A copy in my possession was annotated by Rev. G. W. Stegmann, Sir Bartle Frere's Dutch Secretary (mentioned in 1: 299–300), between the years 1885 and 1891 at the request of Sir Bartle Frere's widow. The note containing this information is tucked into vol.1 between pp. 264–65, and the only pages in vol.1 that have been cut extend from p. 254 to the close (p. 317). It is in a contemporary hand on a slip bearing the Macmillan publisher's watermark.

Stegmann corroborates and rephrases the published account more than he finds occasion to correct it

Chapman and Hall were publishers of *The Fortnightly Review* from 1865, edited among others by Greswell's former schoolmates, T. H. S. Escott and W. L. Courtney. They also published Dickens, Thackeray, Trollope and other fiction writers, as well as The Foreign Library and Library of Travel.

———. "Prize Essay" in *England her Colonies: The Five Best Essays on Imperial Federation submitted to the London Chamber of Commerce*, etc. Adjudged by J. Anthony Froude, J. R. Seeley and Sir Rawson W. Rawson. London: Swan Sonnenschein, Lowrey, 1887. 1–41.

Takes Seeley for granted. Its success may owe much to its low key and modest repetition by one who has direct recent experience.

———. *History of the Dominion of Canada*. Under the Auspices of The Royal Colonial Institute. Oxford: Clarendon Press, 1890.

The Preface states that it is a short study "intended primarily for educational purposes," in schools and for the general reader. Greswell's credentials are advertised on the title page, and the Preface emphasises that the Educational Committee of the Royal Colonial Institute has supervised the putting together of the text. Similar credentials and acknowledgements are cited selectively in subsequent related publications.

———. *Geography of the Dominion of Canada and Newfoundland*. Under the Auspices of The Royal Colonial Institute. Oxford: Clarendon Press, 1890.

As the Preface makes clear, a frankly educational purpose in a format matching the first, history title. The pair of volumes represent for Greswell a lot of homework that broadened and clarified his grasp on the problems of colonisation and federation (compare the 1893 and 1898 publication below).

———. *Tennyson and our Imperial Heritage*. London: Gower, Dodson, 1892a.

———. *Geography of Africa South of the Zambesi: with Notes on the Industries, Wealth, and Social Progress of the States and Peoples*. Under the Auspices of the Royal Colonial Institute. Oxford: Clarendon Press, 1892b.

In the same format as the two 1890 volumes listed above. Appearing after them, and almost fifteen years after Greswell's first book, it was able to look forward more happily to how, "during the next ten years, the various colonies, states, and protectorates gradually settle down" (page vi).

———. *Outlines of British Colonisation...* With an Introduction by the Right Hon. Lord Brassey, K. C. B. London: Percival and Co., 1893.

A skilful expansion and summary of what Greswell knew after more than a decade of research.

———. *The British Colonies and their Industries*. London: Blackie, [1893].

The Preface makes clear that the book was aimed at the classroom. Despite a disparaging review in the *Saturday Review*, 23 April 1898a, it went through six editions by 1905.

116   SELECTED GRESWELL BIBLIOGRAPHY

————. *The Growth and Administration of the British Colonies, 1837–1897.* London: Blackie and Son, 1898b. Victorian Era Series.
The fifth in a series on "the great movements and developments of the age" appearing monthly, priced at 2/6d. Canada receives the largest share, the model of Intercolonial Federation transiting into Imperial Federation ("a triumph of principles"); South Africa receives the least.
————. *The United States and their Industries.* London: G. Philip and Son, 1899. A simple introduction for schools.
————. *The Land of Quantock: A Descriptive and Historical Account.* Taunton: Barnicott and Pearce/Athenæum Press, 1903. 250 numbered copies; with a list of subscribers.
The peculiarities of this book emerge in a comparison with Beatrix F. Creswell's *The Quantock Hills: Their Combes and Villages.* Bristol: William George and Sons, 1904.
————. *The Forests and Deer Parks of the County of Somerset.* Taunton: Barnicott and Pearce/Athenæum Press, 1905. 350 numbered copies; with a list of subscribers.
Flawed by its lack of attention to the larger, Devonian context.
————. *Admiral Blake: General-at-Sea.* Bridgwater, Somerset: Page and Son, 1907.
My copy, in wrappers, is inscribed to Henry Francis Cheetham of Triscombe House, near West Bagborough, and accompanied by a letter from Greswell dated 22 December 1906.
————. *Chapters on the Early History of Glastonbury Abbey.* Taunton: Barnicott and Pearce/The Wessex Press, 1909. 500 copies, not numbered; with a list of subscribers.
Draws attention to the many Celtic associations of the old Abbey.
————. *The Story of the Battle of Edington.* Taunton: Barnicott and Pearce/The Wessex Press, 1910. With a list of subscribers.
The basis of Alfred's campaigns against the Vikings, which Greswell drew upon in his final book (1922.)
————. A worn, black-covered manuscript notebook with "W. H. GRESWELL." embossed in gold caps. on the top cover. "<For> Kilve Library 1917," handwritten on a white slip pasted above. Somerset Archives and Local Studies, Southwest Heritage Trust, Somerset Heritage Centre, Brunel Way, Norton Fitzwarren, Taunton TA2 65F. Reference no. "DD/CWC. bw/13 (Greswell 1917)", also on a white slip pasted onto the cover.
The listing was begun in November 1917, completed in January 1918, and fills roughly 90 pages written on both sides. It describes the books as they are arranged in bookcases in Greswell's Minehead house as he hoped to have them transported to Kilve. They are arranged under three main categories—Somerset and County archaeology and natural history, Opera Greswelliana, and the

author's father's library—although the organisation is in practice very confused. They nonetheless supply many small details in my account.

———. *Dumnonia and The Valley of the Parret: A Historical Retrospect.* Taunton: Barnicott and Pearce/The Wessex Press, 1922. With a list of subscribers.
Further thoughts and revised opinions on Greswell's later work.

Griggs, Earl Leslie (ed.). *Unpublished Letters of Samuel Taylor Coleridge.* 2 vols. London: Constable, 1932.

Grundlingh, M. A. S. "The Diary of George William Stegmann (1844–1891)" *Quarterly Bulletin of the South African Library* 43 (1989): 123–31, 160–66.
Stegmann, a minister of the Dutch Reformed Church, accompanied Sir Bartle Frere as secretary and translator during the latter's time as High Commissioner for South Africa, and he corrected my copy of Greswell's *Our South African Empire* at Lady Frere's request, covering the beginning of the Anglo-Zulu War. Greswell refers to Stegmann apropos the same topic, the most controversial episode in Frere's African career (*Our South African Empire* 1: 229–330, 304–05). See also, John Martineau *Life and Correspondence of Sir Bartle Frere.* Chap. 19.

Hagerman, C. *Britain's Imperial Muse: The Classics, Imperialism, and the Indian Empire.* London: Palgrave Macmillan, 2013.
Three references to Greswell.

Harvey, Samantha C. *Transatlantic Transcendentalism: Coleridge, Emerson, and Nature.* Edinburgh: Edinburgh UP, 2013. Edinburgh Studies in Transatlantic Literatures.

Haven, Richard, Josephine Haven, and Maurianne Adams. *Samuel Taylor Coleridge: An Annotated Bibliography of Criticism and Scholarship. Volume I: 1793–1899.* Boston, MA: G. K. Hall, 1976. See also Walter B. Crawford.

Hazlitt, William. *The Complete Works of William Hazlitt.* Ed. P. P. Howe. 21 vols. London: J. M. Dent and Sons, 1930–34.

Hesketh, Ian. *Victorian Jesus: J. R. Seeley, Religion, and the Cultural Significance of Anonymity.* Toronto, ON: University of Toronto Press, 2017.
The title advertises the theme of anonymity and how it was exploited by Seeley and his publisher. At the same time, the book discusses the relation between the themes of all Seeley's publications and has a useful bibliography.

Hirst, Francis. *A Man of Principle: The Life of Percy Alport Molteno. M. P.* Chapters of Hirst's unpublished biography of Molteno, the typescript completed in 1939, now at University of Cape Town Archives, prepared by Robert Molteno. Online at <http://www.moltenofamily.net/wp-content/uploads/2013/12/Introduction-selected-chapters.pdf> accessed 7 November 2018.
Includes Greswell among Molteno's grateful memories of masters at Diocesan College (p. 12), and provides a fascinating insight into lives lived by those with whom Greswell came into close contact.

118 SELECTED GRESWELL BIBLIOGRAPHY

Holmes, Edmond. *Selected Poetry and Prose*. Ed. John Howlett. Madison, WI: Fairleigh Dickinson UP, 2016.

Hort, F. J. A. "Coleridge" in *Cambridge Essays, contributed by Members of the University*. London: John W. Parker, 1856: 292–351.

The essay that challenges James Martineau's, published during the same year, for the position of the best single essay on Coleridge's thinking, albeit from a younger man's point of view.

Houghton, Walter E., *et al.* (eds.). *The Wellesley Index to Victorian Periodicals, 1824–1900*. 5 vols. Toronto, ON: University of Toronto Press, 1966–1987.

Identifies thirty-two essays contributed by Greswell to six journals. There are perhaps twenty more.

Howlett, John. *Edmond Holmes and Progressive Education*. Abingdon, Oxon: Routledge, 2017.

Conservative St. John"s College, Oxon, as a background against which to rebel.

Howsam, Leslie. "Imperial Publishers and the Idea of Colonial History, 1870–1916." *History of Intellectual Culture* 5 (2005): 1–15. Online at <http://www.ucalgary.ca/hic • ISSN 1492-7810> accessed 15 October 2018). The background to the publication of Seeley's lectures, how they were recommended to the publisher Macmillan, and their success. Oxford UP attempted to find authors on colonial imperialism following the success of Seeley's *Expansion* (1883). Greswell did not come to mind at the time or in the decade later, but he was employed to write schoolbooks.

Ingram, Brian. "Evangelicalism and Religious Crisis: The Experience of George Eliot." In *Spiritual Identities: Literature and the Post-Secular Imagination*. Ed. Jo Carruthers and Andrew Tate. Bern, Switzerland: Peter Lang, 2010. 49–64. Describes the "Rosehill Circle" at Coventry, which formed around Caroline and Charles Bray, Charles Hennell and Dr. R. H. Brabant's daughter Rufa. It involved Mary Ann Evans and other prominent mid-century freethinkers: a context that bears significantly on the interpretation of the items chosen to open Greswell's collection.

Jackson. J. R. de J., ed. *Coleridge: The Critical Heritage*. 2 vols. London: Routledge, 1970–91.

[Jowett, Benjamin, *et al.*]: see Shea and Whitla (eds.). *Essays and Reviews* (1860).

Kennedy, William F. *Humanist verses Economist: The Economic Thought of Samuel Taylor Coleridge*. Berkeley, CA: University of California Press, 1958.

A book often overlooked: e.g. by Philip Aherne.

Kilcrease, Bethany. *The Great Church Crisis and the End of English Erastianism, 1898–1906*. Abingdon, Oxon: Routledge, 2016.

Greswell cited on pp. 112 and 120 re. his 1900 *Fortnightly Review* article that argues Dutch clergy fomented war.

Knox, Bruce A. "The Rise of Colonial Federation as an Object of British Policy, 1850–1870." *Journal of British Studies* 11 (November 1971): 92–112.

Lockridge, Laurence S. "The Coleridge Circle: Virtue Ethics, Sympathy, and Outrage." *Humantitas* (Washington, DC) 29: 1 & 2 (2016); 43–78.
A wide-ranging and suggestive review of how the concept of Virtue Ethics applies to the work of several Romantic authors.

Longson, Patrick. *The Rise of the German Menace: Imperial Anxiety and British Popular Culture, 1896–1903.* PhD University of Birmingham, 2013. Online at <http://etheses.bham.ac.uk/5094/2/Longson14PhD_Redacted.pdf> accessed 26 October 2018.
Cites several periodical essays by Greswell published during the 1890s on Germany as a surreptitious and menacing colonising power.

Lysiak, Arthur Walter. *T. H. S. Escott: Victorian Journalist.* Loyola University Chicago Ph D Disssertation, 1970. <http://ecommons.luc/edu/luc_diss/1038> accessed 8 November 2018.
See Lysiak Part 1, Chap. 2 on Escott's newspaper campaign against Salisbury during the time Greswell was at the Cape; and Part 2, Chap. 3 on Escott's views on Empire and Federation.

McIntyre, Donald. *The Diocesan College, Rondebosch, South Africa: A Century of "Bishops".* Cape Town: Juta, 1950.
Greswell must have prepared Percy Molteno and helped him attain his excellent matriculation result when he left school in 1878 (see pp. 24 fn2 and p. 84). The book reveals (p. 24) that "professors" (teachers at the senior school) were paid £200 a year by the government (roughly £11,000 at today's value).
See also, *South African Empire* 2: 276–77 instructing the Kafir in Greek declensions, "in my capacity as Government Lecturer." See also 2: 290 on tutoring a Kafir at Gill College, Somerset East. There is evidence that Greswell taught at both Rondebosch (Bishop's) and Somerset East (Gill College) during the same year (1877).

McKillop, A. B. (ed.). *A Critical Spirit: The Thought of William Dawson LeSueur.* Toronto, ON: McLelland and Stewart in association with the Institute of Canadian Studies, Carleton University. The Carleton Library, 104.
W. D. LeSueur (1840–1917), Anglo-Canadian intellectual who shared many of the same advanced positions as Greswell's Oxford friend Boodle and published in the same journals. The quickening sense of critical enquiry in Upper Canada and Montreal at the time contrasts with Greswell's relatively isolated experience at the Cape.

———. *A Disciplined Intelligence: Critical Inquiry and Canadian Thought in the Victorian Era.* Montreal: McGill-Queen's UP, 1979; reprinted as Carleton Library Series 193 in 2001.
Describes the intellectual situation Boodle found when he arrived in Toronto as a teacher of Classics. But what was Boodle doing between 1881 and 1886, when he is to be found living in Montreal? Did he move to Montreal and gain the managerial experience that helped him gain the Fraser-Hickson Library job?

120   SELECTED GRESWELL BIBLIOGRAPHY

McLachlan, H. *The Story of a Nonconformist Library.* Manchester: Manchester UP, 1923.

Pages 2–4 describe a manuscript catalogue begun in 1875 by W. E. A. Axon; completed by James Black and J. Edwin Odgers (both tutors of the Board, later College). In 1888, Odgers, by now Principal of the College, was also appointed Librarian (he was succeeded by Alexander Gordon as both Principal and Librarian in 1890). Axon (1846–1913) published on Coleridge, among his many other interests. Could he or Odgers, whom Greswell evidently knew, have helped to assemble the Coleridge materials?

Major, Albany F. *Early Wars of Wessex: being Studies from England's School of Arms in the West.* Ed. Charles W. Whistler. Cambridge: Cambridge UP, 1913.

A book that engages with Greswell's recent histories of the area at several points, benefitting from his local knowledge.

Mallock, W. H. *The New Republic: Culture, Faith and Philosophy in an English Country House* (1877, rev 1879). Ed. John Lucas. Leicester: Leicester UP, 1975.

The novel circulated in manuscript and as a topic of discussion in Oxford university circles before a version was published anonymously in *Belgravia: An Illustrated Monthly Magazine* in seven monthly parts (June-December 1876): that is, at the time Greswell was leaving for South Africa. His friend Boodle used it as the text on which to centre his description of spiritual crisis in a series of articles in a Toronto journal a few years later (see above).

Martineau, James. *A Study of Religion, Its Sources and Contents.* Oxford: Clarendon Press, 1888.

Martineau criticizes Seeley's *Natural Religion* as a book that fails to acknowledge the personal and moral relationship between the human soul and God at 2: 353. See also, *Life and Letters.* 2: 416–17.

———. *Essays, Reviews and Addresses.* 4 vols. London: Longmans, Green, 1890–91.

"The National Church as a Federal Union" (at 2: 539–76), which began as a lecture, was first published in *The Contemporary Review*, March 1887, and as separate pamphlet in about September of the same year. See *Life and Letters* 2: 108–128 for the background of the proposal.

———. *Life and Letters.* Ed. James Drummond and C. B. Upton. 2 vols. London: James Nisbet, 1902.

In March 1869, Henry Sidgwick became Vice-President of James Martineau's campaign to create a "Free Christian Union" (1: 435). The Union was dissolved in December 1870.

Martineau, John. *Life and Correspondence of Sir Bartle Frere.* 2 vols. London: John Murray, 1895.

Mendelssohn, Sidney. *Mendelssohn's South African Bibliography.* Introd. I. D. Colvin. 2 vols. London: Kegan Paul, Trench, Trübner, 1910.

Lists besides the obvious (*Fortnightly Review, National Review*, etc.) many lesser magazines Greswell contributed to as he exhausted what he had to say about South Africa.

Miall, David S. "The Campaign to Acquire Coleridge Cottage." *The Wordsworth Circle* 22: 1 (1991): 82–88.

The first version of the article was published in *The Coleridge Bulletin* No.1 (1988). The expanded version is available at online@sites.ualberta.ca~dmiall/ Essays/ColeridgeCottage.htm#views. Document prepared 19 March 2003; accessed 18 October 2021.

[Mill, John Stuart.] "Bentham." *Westminster Review* 29 (August 1838): 467–506. Slightly revised version in Mill's *Dissertations and Discussions* (2 vols. London: John W. Parker, 1859) 1: 330–92; see also *Collected Works, Volume 10: Essays on Ethics, Religion and Society* ed. John M. Robson, F. E. L. Priestley and D. P. Dryer (Toronto, ON: University of Toronto Press, 1985). 75–115.

[———.] "Coleridge." *Westminster Review* 33 (March 1840): 257–302. Slightly revised version in Mill's *Dissertations and Discussions* ((2 vols. London: John W. Parker, 1859) 1: 393–466; see also *Collected Works, Volume 10: Essays on Ethics, Religion and Society* ed. John M. Robson, F. E. L. Priestley and D. P. Dryer (Toronto, ON: University of Toronto Press, 1985). 117–63.

Molteno, Percy Alport. *Selections from the Correspondence of Percy Alport Molteno, 1892–1914.* Ed. Vivian Solomon. Cape Town: Van Riebeeck Society, 1981.

Includes Greswell's letter on pp. 24–25, from Bridgwater dated 20 April 1896, thanking Molteno for his recent book, *A Federal South Africa*, and politely but frankly disagreeing with it.

Monsman, Gerald. *Walter Pater.* Boston, MA: Twayne Publishers, 1977. Twayne's English Authors series, 207.

Moodey, Edgar C. *The Fraser-Hickson Library: An Informal History.* London: Clive Bingley, 1977. For The Fraser-Hickson Institute.

Appendix IV list of Officers gives Boodle's term as Secretary and Chief Librarian as 1886–1897 (p. 212). During the crucial formative years of the library, "Boodle proved highly efficient both as a librarian and as a business agent" (p. 72). However, p. 78 has it that "Towards the end of 1890 the librarian, R. W. Boodle, had also retired, to return to Birmingham, England, and in his place Eugène Malcouronne had been appointed." Moodey describes circumstances surrounding the 1886 and 1890 dates, so one must assume 1897 on p. 212 to be a misprint. Basically, Boodle played an important role in the foundation years of the new library.

Morris, Jeremy. *F. D. Maurice and the Crisis of Christian Authority.* Oxford: Oxford UP, 2005. Christian Theology in Context series.

[Mozley, John Rickards.] "Coleridge as a Poet." Review of *Poems of Samuel Taylor Coleridge* ed. Derwent Coleridge and Sara Coleridge, 1854. *Quarterly Review* 125 (1868): 78–106.

[———.] Cumulative review of Tennyson, Browning, Mrs. Browning, Clough and Arnold entitled "Modern English Poets" in *Quarterly Review* 126 (April 1869): 328–59.

122   SELECTED GRESWELL BIBLIOGRAPHY

[————.] Review of Sidgwick *Methods of Ethics* entitled "Utilitarianism and Morality" in *Quarterly Review* 141 (1876): 488–506.

Nichols, W[illiam] L[uke]. *The Quantocks and their Associations; A Paper read before the Members of the Bath Literary Club on the 11th December 1871.* Bath: Printed for Private Circulation, 1873.

A second edition, "Revised and Enlarged, with Map and Eleven Illustrations," was published by Sampson Low, Marston, and Co., in 1891. A copy of this edition was also published on large paper, limited to 200 copies.

Odgers, J. Edwin. Introduction to *Ecce Homo* by John Robert Seeley (first published 1866). London: George Routledge and Sons, 1910. Books that Marked Epochs series, 8.

Odgers was a prominent Unitarian with West country connections who lived on the Woodstock Road near Richard Greswell's daughters at the time he subscribed to Greswell's *Land of Quantock*. In his Introduction (p. xxiv), he points out how Seeley's "Christ placed the happiness of man in 'a political constitution'. Again, he [Seeley] calls it 'the Christian commonwealth'." (And here Odgers' footnote refers to *Ecce Homo* chaps. 9–14, 17.) Odgers closes his introduction by emphasizing the message of moral behaviour, readjustment of social obligations, and undertaking of new responsibilities. He quotes Seeley's 1867 lecture: "the Christian Church is bound to have a philosophy of society." [Is this the connection with the colonial argument, the universal commonwealth?]

Palen, Marc William. "Adam Smith as Advocate of Empire, c.1870–1932." *The Historical Journal* (Cambridge) 57 (March 2014): 179–98.

Pages 189–90 put Greswell into context as an advocate of imperial federation contra the Manchester School and the ruling Cobdenite opposition; also the Canadian context of the debate.

Pater, Walter. "Coleridge" in his *Appreciations, with an Essay on Style*. London: Macmillan, 1889. 64–106 (64–81 esp.).

Combines the extensively revised version of Pater's *Westminster Review* essay with his essay on Coleridge's poetry written for Thomas Humphry Ward's anthology of *English Poets* (Macmillan 1880). The *Westminster* essay was not republished in its original form during Pater's lifetime.

Plug, Cornelis. "Greswell, Reverend William Henry Parr (geography, ornithology)." S2A3 Biographical Database of Southern African Science. Online at <https://www.s2a3.org.za/bio/Biograph_final.php?serial=1145> accessed 7 July 2018.

Notes Greswell's education at Somersetshire College, Bath, and "From 1876 to 1884 he was a lecturer of classics and English literature under the Higher Education Act of the Cape Colony." Interesting that Plug classifies him as a scientist on the basis of his exact descriptions of flora.

SELECTED GRESWELL BIBLIOGRAPHY 123

Porter, Dennis. *A Catalogue of Manuscripts in Harris Manchester College*. Oxford: Harris Manchester College, PDF 1998 updated 2015 <www.hmc.ox.ac/library/specialcollections>, accessed 31 November 2018.

Prickett, Stephen. *Romanticism and Religion: The Tradition of Coleridge and Wordsworth in the Victorian Church*. Cambridge: Cambridge UP, 1976.

Another version of a familiar story. It allows more space to Keble, ends with Arnold and MacDonald ("Demythologising and Myth-Making"), and traces a literary version of religious imagination.

Raugh, Harold E. *Anglo-Zulu War, 1879: A Selected Bibliography*. Lanham, MD: Scarecrow Press, 2011.

Reardon, Bernard M. G. *From Coleridge to Gore: A Century of Religious Thought in Britain*. London: Longman, 1971.

An older standard history that retains its value. James Martineau is discussed under the heading Personal Idealism on pp. 312–15.

Reeder, W. T. "The Revd. W. H. P. Greswell, F.R.G.S." *Proceedings of the Somerset Archaeological Society and Natural History Society* 68 (1922): 122–23.

A couple of small errors but entirely fitting; that is, it gives nothing away.

Ritchie, W. *The History of the South African College, 1829–1918*. 2 vols. Capetown: T. Maskew Miller, 1918.

Founded in 1829, with mixed (Dutch-English) beginnings; the campus was at Newlands, now an adjacent suburb of Stellenbosch (the location of Diocesan College/Bishop's, founded 1849). South African College (SAC) was larger, more mixed in intake, and more muddled in organisation than Bishop's. The two other South African schools competing at the time were the Paul Roos Gymnasium, Stellenbosch (founded 1866, Afrikaans tradition) and St Andrews College, Grahamstown (founded by an Anglican bishop in 1855)—this latter pair in Western Province.

How different would Greswell's perspective have been if he had been attached to one of the other colleges?

Robbins, William. *The Ethical Idealism of Matthew Arnold: A Study of the Nature and Sources of his Moral and Religious Ideas*. Toronto, ON: University of Toronto Press, 1959.

Arnold was a significant spokesperson on religious matters during Greswell's time at Oxford. He did not write at length on Coleridge, but he is part of the subtext in Greswell's inclusion of Pater's "review" (item **36**).

Rutherford, Mark [William Hale White]. *The Autobiography of Mark Rutherford* [1881] *and Mark Rutherford's Deliverance: Edited by his Friend, Reuben Shapcott*. 2nd ed., corr. with addns. London: Trübner, 1888.

———. *Catharine Furze. Edited by his Friend, Reuben Shapcott*. 2 vols. London: T. Fisher Unwin, 1893.

———. *More Pages from a Journal, with Other Papers*. London: Henry Frowde/Oxford UP, 1910.

124 SELECTED GRESWELL BIBLIOGRAPHY

Contains "Extracts from a Diary in the Quantocks" on pp. 186–204 (dated at head of text "Spring 18—"; and see White's *Letters to Three Friends*. 182–85, which confirms the visit took place in 1899). There is high praise for "Love's First Hope" as matching Coleridge's Stowey days in quality on pp. 194–95. White discussed the poem with Ernest Hartley Coleridge shortly before he died, in 1913: Dorothy V. White. *The Groombridge Diary*. London: Humphrey Milford/Oxford UP, 1924. 465–66.

————. *Letters to Three Friends*. London: Humphrey Milford/Oxford UP, 1924.

Sandford, Mrs. Henry. *Thomas Poole and his Friends*. 2 vols. London: Macmillan, 1888.

Mrs. Sandford was born Margaret Poole, and her father was Thomas Poole's cousin.

Schneewind, J. B. *Sidgwick's Ethics and Victorian Moral Philosophy*. Oxford: Clarendon Press, 1977.

A classic study of the major philosopher among the Cambridge moralists, with sections on Coleridge and the Coleridgeans (Chap. 3). Of particular interest in the present context are the pages on Sidgwick and Seeley (28–35, 45–46), and Act and Agency in Sidgwick and James Martineau (Chap. 8).

[Seeley, John Robert.] *Ecce Homo: A Survey of the Life and Work of Jesus Christ*. London, 1866 [*vere* 1865]: see above J. Edwin Odgers.

The book caused a storm of discussion when it was published. Seeley refused to acknowledge his authorship for a long time, although it soon became widely known.

————. *Lectures and Essays*. London: Macmillan, 1870.

Seeley forcefully expressed his respect for Coleridge as a systematic thinker in the essay on "Milton's Political Opinions" (pp. 98–99), which first appeared in *Macmillan's Magazine* February 1868.

[————.] *Natural Religion*. London: Macmillan, 1882.

Four instalments, all entitled "The Deeper Harmonies of Science and Religion," appeared between May and December 1875 of *Popular Science Monthly*; and, as the Preface points out, the book began as a series of articles in *Macmillan's Magazine* between 1875 and 1878. My own copy was extensively annotated over three days in August 1882 by John Whale (1863–1916), who was a lay preacher among the Free Methodists of Cornwall and entered the Congregational ministry in 1901. He found the book "most suggestive and full of interest," but wished the concluding remarks that dismiss supernaturalism had been omitted. Seeley specifically defended his argument against supernaturalism in the preface to a second edition that appeared later the same year (1882).

————. *The Expansion of England* [1883]. Ed. John Gross. Chicago: The University of Chicago Press, 1971. Classics of British Historical Literature series. An important book in the earlier stages of Greswell's career.

SELECTED GRESWELL BIBLIOGRAPHY 125

Shea, Victor, and William Whitla (eds.). *Essays and Reviews: The 1860 Text and its Readings*. Charlottesville, VA: University of Virginia Press, 2000.

Short, Edward. *Newman and his Family*. London: Bloomsbury, 2013.

Chapter 8, "John Rickards Mozley and Late Victorian Scepticism" (pp. 327–79), provides a summary life and draws upon Mozley's correspondence on spiritual matters with his two maternal uncles, John Henry Newman and Francis William Newman, the latter of whom rejected biblical authority and Christian dogma. Short also makes connections with Clough and Arnold, and later nineteenth-century Cambridge movements of thought (Coleridge mediated by Maurice, Grote, Sidgwick, Seeley and Marshall, in particular).

Shute, Chris. *Edmond Holmes and "The Tragedy of Education"*. Nottingham: Educational Heretics Press, 1998.

Slote, Michael. *Morals from Motives*. Oxford: Oxford University Press, 2001.

An attempt to revive an interest in agent-based virtue ethics with particular reference to James Martineau, among others. Such an idea is vital to Coleridge's own self-justification, despite the intellectual difficulties it caused him.

Smuts, F. "Classical Scholarship and the Teaching of Classics at Cape Town and Stellenbosch." *Acta Classica: Proceedings of the Classical Association of South Africa* 3 (January 1960): 7–31.

No mention of Greswell.

Staunton, Howard. *The Great Schools of England. New Edition, Revised and Corrected; with an Appendix, containing Notices of the Endowed Grammar Schools of England and Wales*. London: Strahan, 1869.

First published by Sampson Low, Son and Marston in 1865, without the Appendix on p. 557 which provides the details of Somersetshire College Bath. The 1869 volume was reprinted in 1877 by Daldy, Isbister, of London without revision: that is, in particular, without recording further honours won by students at the college in the intervening eight years.

Stegmann, George William. *Diary*, 13 December 1878–10 March 1879: see above M. A. S. Grundlingh.

Note that the diary begins on the day following Frere's "famous ultimatum" of 12 December 1878: see Greswell *Our South African Empire* 1: 302.

Stone, Wilfred. *Religion and Art of William Hale White ("Mark Rutherford")*. Stanford, CA: Stanford UP, 1954.

References to what Hale White likes and dislikes in Coleridge on pp. 24, 65, 66, 66n. Close to Greswell in dislike of Coleridge's German metaphysics and later orthodoxy and instead values the "Ancient Mariner" and "Christabel" or specific literary aperçus. Wordsworth's "God of the hills" (and Goethe and Carlyle) are held to be more important.

Taylor, J. Glen. "'Miss Greswell Honed our Hebrew at Oxford': Reflections on Joanna J. Greswell and her Book *Grammatical Analysis of the Hebrew Psalter* (1873)." In *Breaking Boundaries: Female Biblical Interpreters Who Challenged*

126 SELECTED GRESWELL BIBLIOGRAPHY

the Status Quo. Ed. Nancy Calvert-Koyzis and Heather Weir. T. & T. Clark: New York, 2010. 85–106.

Joanna Greswell was William Greswell's cousin (Uncle Richard's daughter), who lived on the Woodstock Road, Oxford, and subscribed to his books while she was alive.

Thompson, David M. *Cambridge Theology in the Nineteenth Century: Enquiry, Controversy and Truth*. Aldershot, Hants: Ashgate, 2008.

Chapter 4 "The Coleridgean Inheritance" covers Coleridge's influence on Connop Thirlwall, Julius Hare and F. D. Maurice (viz. up to mid-century). Little is said about Unitarians and Transcendentalists.

See separately for Coleridge's larger influence on later nineteenth-century Cambridge intellectuals like Grote, Sidgwick, Seeley, Marshall, Mozley. And compare the Oxford story during the interval between the novels of J. A. Froude and Mrs. Humphrey Ward (Tractarians, etc.; *Essays and Reviews* 1860, M. Arnold), which was more irregular and "literary."

Traill, H. D. "A Pious Legend Examined." *Fortnightly Review* new series 37 (1885): 223–33.

A reply to Tulloch in ibid 37 (January 1885): 11–25 = Greswell item **32**.

Trezise, Simon. *The West Country as a Literary Invention: Putting Fiction in its Place*. Exeter: University of Exeter Press, 2000.

Ungureanu, James. C. "Edward Livingston Youmans and the 'Peacemakers' in the Popular Science Monthly." *Fides et Historia* 51:2 (2019) 13–32.

The North American context of Boodle's review of Seeley's *Natural Religion* (1882).

Walker, Eric A. *The South African College and the University of Cape Town: Written for the University Centenary Celebration*. Cape Town: Cape Times for the University of Cape Town, 1929.

Add to Ritchie (above), but no mention of Greswell.

Walters, Ray Charlotte (comp.). *A Catalogue and Index of the Letters to Ernest Hartley Coleridge*. PhD dissertation, University of Texas at Austin, submitted August 1971. University Microfilms International facsimile no.72–15, 818.

As the full title says, summaries and quotations from numerous letters to Ernest Coleridge, the originals all now under the call number Ms | Coleridge EH | Misc. The authors I refer to are Wathen Call; Kegan Paul (two letters concerning the letters in Call's hands); William Greswell (eight letters written between 14 August 1893 and 18 September 1915); William Knight; and finally (not included in Walters but under the same call number) William Greswell to James Dykes Campbell, 17 July 1893.

Ward, Mrs. Humphry. *Robert Elsmere* (1888). Ed. Rosemary Ashton. Oxford: Oxford UP, 1987. The World's Classics.

The author was a niece of Matthew Arnold and the origins of her novel lay in her reaction to the strongly orthodox Bampton Lecture of 1881 given by John

SELECTED GRESWELL BIBLIOGRAPHY   127

Wordsworth, great-nephew of the poet and fellow of Brasenose since 1867. The book challenged dogmatic Christianity, caused considerable controversy and was a bestseller of its day in Britain and North America.

———. *A Writer's Recollections.* 2 vols. New York: Harper and Brothers, 1918.

Watts, Michael R. "'The ground on which Rational Christianity may firmly take its stand': Higher Criticism and the Unitarians." In his *The Dissenters, Volume III. The Crisis and Conscience of Nonconformity.* Oxford: Clarendon Press, 2015. 20–27.

On the brilliance and ultimate failure of James Martineau's attempt to shift the basis of religion from external evidence to internal conscience.

Webb, Philip. *The Letters of Philip Webb.* Ed. John Aplin. 4 vols. London: Routledge, 2016. 3: 29.

In a letter dated 7 June 1889, Webb asks William Hale White "if the place [sc. the north-east side of the Quantocks] is overrun in the summer time with various minded tourists."

White, William Hale: *see above* Mark Rutherford

Wigmore-Beddoes, Dennis G. *Yesterday's Radicals: A Study of the Affinity between Unitarianism and Broad Church Anglicanism in the Nineteenth Century.* Cambridge: James Clarke, 1971.

The "affinity" bears on the return to the Unitarian connection that recurs through Greswell's Coleridge book. NB the coincidence of Coleridge's father's interests: namely, his local friendships, and his choice of a Unitarian godfather for his son.

Beside the general point advertised in the subtitle, useful for (a) the evolution of a liberal understanding from Thomas Arnold and going back to seventeenth-century Latitudinarians; (b) the Jowett quote on how "every great and good man is inspired"; (c) James Martineau, the nineteenth-century Unitarian and his connection with Maurice; (d) how Pater's ordination was obstructed by his study of Maurice; (e) Sidgwick as Vice-President of Martineau's Free Christian Union 1870 (*Life* 1: 435), and (f) Martineau's "National Church as a Federal Union" 1887 (*Essays Reviews etc.* 2: 567)

Willey, Basil. *Nineteenth Century Studies: Coleridge to Matthew Arnold.* London: Chatto and Windus, 1949.

The main line of theological debate, beginning with a chapter on Coleridge, constructed for undergraduate students of literature seventy years ago.

———. *More Nineteenth Century Studies: A Group of Honest Doubters.* London: Chatto and Windus, 1956.

A study that attempts to "fill in some of the gaps [sc. in Willey's 1949 book] and bring the story down to the end of the century" (p. 5) and in which Coleridge is again prominent.

White, William Hale: *see above* Mark Rutherford.

128 SELECTED GRESWELL BIBLIOGRAPHY

Wordsworth, Dorothy. *The Grasmere and Alfoxden Journals.* Edited by Pamela Woof. Oxford: Oxford UP, 2002. Oxford World's Classics.

Wormell, Deborah. *Sir John Seeley and the Uses of History.* Cambridge: Cambridge UP, 1980.
Discusses the influence of Coleridge and Maurice, and the idea of a Broad Church as liberation.

Yoshikawa, Saeko. *William Wordsworth and the Invention of Tourism, 1820–1900.* Farnham, Surrey: Ashgate, 2014.

Young, David. *F. D. Maurice and Unitarianism.* Oxford: Clarendon Press, 1992.
A book particularly useful for the way it traces the evolution of nineteenth-century Unitarianism away from its late eighteenth-century beginnings—represented by Priestley, Thomas Belsham, and William Frend—that is, the context most familiar to students of early Coleridge—to the different kind of religion represented by F. D. Maurice, James Martineau and others, which is much closer to the mainspring of Coleridge's mature theology (of course, with most important exceptions besides).

Index[1]

A

American transcendentalism
and culture
  Carlyle's connections with
    but more personalised
    quarrel with Coleridge,
    4, 85
  more fully developed than its
    British counterpart,
    76, 78–82
  used skilfully to clarify an
    outside view of the main
    argument, 2
Arnold, Matthew, 37, 68, 71, 83,
    84, 97, 98
  representative of Oxford
    conservatives for Greswell,
    68, 71, 83, 84, 97
  uncle of Mrs Humphry Ward, 37

B

Ball, Sir Alexander (1757–1809), 73
  The "truly great man" who
    occupied the same place in
    Coleridge's mind as Sir Bartle
    Frere in Greswell's, 73
Boodle, Richard William (1850–1918),
    70–72, 84, 85, 97, 99, 100
  an adventurous and organised
    intellect, 85
  librarian in Montreal and later
    Birmingham, 85
  lifelong friendship with Greswell,
    70, 73, 84, 85, 99
  particular interest in contemporary
    religious thinking, 70, 85
  possibly influenced the argument of
    the second part of Greswell's
    book, 86

---

[1] Note: Page numbers followed by 'n' refer to notes.

© The Author(s), under exclusive license to Springer Nature
Switzerland AG 2023
J. C. C. Mays, *Coleridge in William Greswell's Workbook*,
https://doi.org/10.1007/978-3-031-38593-3

130 INDEX

Brabant, Robert Herbert
(1781?–1866), 47, 78, 79
free-thinking medical doctor and
friend of Coleridge, practising
at Bath in 1815–16; later a core
member of the freethinking
"Rosehill Circle" at
Coventry, 78
Brabant, Rufa (properly Elizabeth
Rebecca) (1811–1898), 78, 79
daughter of Dr R. H. Brabant;
married Charles Hennell and
later Wathen Call; began the
English translation of Strauss's
Das Leben Jesu, which was
completed by George Eliot;
member of the "Rosehill
Circle," 78, 79

C

Call, Wathen (1817–1890), 47,
79, 81, 102
second husband of Rufa Brabant:
author of Reverberations
(1876) and items 2 and 3 in
Greswell's book, 78, 79
Cambridge, University of, vi, 31, 69,
74, 77, 81, 84
its nineteenth-century status contra
Oxford, 69
Campbell, James Dykes (1838–1895),
52, 61, 78, 97
Coleridge scholar, 52
Carlyle, Thomas (1795–1881), v, 4, 6,
26, 39, 67, 73, 78, 78n1, 79,
81–86, 98, 101–105
particular relevance of his *Life of
Sterling* (1851), v, 78
promotor of "natural
supernaturalism," 83, 101, 102
"Try it", 94–95

Coleridge, Ernest Hartley (1846–1920),
5, 79, 91, 92, 94, 97
correspondence with
Greswell, 92–94
disinclination to advertise his uncle's
letters to Brabant, 77
instrumental in purchase of
Coleridge's Stowey home, 94
Coleridge's present reputation
"Ancient Mariner" always
remembered, 43, 58
intelligent commentary, 121–122
Stowey poet, 3, 4, 43, 46,
61, 92–94
Collected Coleridge
its aim to finish the job Sara and
Henry Nelson Coleridge
began, 48
Craik, George Lillie (1798–1866), 106
as a critic of Coleridge's poetry,
106, 109–110

E

Eliot, George, 78
See also Mary Anne Evans
Evans, Mary Ann (1819–1880), 78
friend of Rufa Brabant, 78

F

Frere, John Hookham (1769–1846)
uncle of Henry Bartle Frere ; his
translations of Aristophanes
admired by Coleridge, 111
Frere, Sir Henry Bartle (1815–1884),
53, 73, 88, 89, 91
after a successful career in India
lasting thirty years, appointed
Governor and High
Commissioner to South Africa
in 1877, 73, 88

INDEX 131

Greswell's respect for, 53, 73, 88
recalled to England in 1880, 88
a series of disastrous events and lack
   of practical support for,
   88–89, 112
See also Stegman, Rev. G. W.
Froude, James Anthony (1818–1904),
   37, 38, 73, 88, 97
author of *Oceana: or England and
   her Colonies* (1886), 112
author of *The Nemesis of Faith*
   (1849), 37

G

Gladstone, William Ewart
   (1809–1898), 68, 88
friend of Richard Greswell, 88
Greswell, William Henry Parr
   (1848–1923), 56–61, 64–71,
   76–80, 82–86, 88–94, 96–103,
   105, 106
his career as a writer and final book,
   88, 88n1, 90–92, 100
his career as Coleridge secretary
   follows a predictable pattern,
   ending with a list of books and
   vain hopes for a Wordsworth
   library at Aldenham House,
   Kilve, 94
family influences on, 96–98
at large, 98–100
an Oxford education but events at
   Cambridge intellectually more
   interesting (*see* Mozley, John
   Rickards; Seeley, John; Arnold,
   Matthew; Pater, Walter)
Oxford friendships (*see* Boodle,
   Richard; Holmes, Edmond)
why South Africa and colonial
   confederation?, 5, 70, 98, 99

Greswell's Coleridge Workbook
   annotations/sources in blue and
      black pencil, 11
anomalies in the contents list, 21–25
bound by C. T. Jefferies & Sons in
   1884 or after, 9; later insertoin
   of five items, 10
changes hands; dispersed via Bristol
   bookshop in 1920s, 8; at rest in
   University of Limerick, Special
   Collections, vi
mistakes in attributing sources, 14, 24
phases of book's composition;
   separate pages from various
   sources, 16, 18; some items
   positioned with care, 29–33
reader's markings, 24

H

Harris Manchester College Oxford, 20
   See also Martineau, James, Professor
      of Mental and Moral
      Philosophy and Political
      Economy from 1840 to 1885
Hazlitt, William (1778–1830)
   young admirer who became fierce
      critic of Coleridge, 4, 39,
      47, 52, 53
Hennell, Charles (1800–1850), 78, 79
   author of *Inquiry concerning the
      Origin of Christianity*
      (1838), 78
   married Rufa Brabant in
      1843, 78, 79
Holmes, Edmond (1850–1936)
   Oxford friend of Greswell and
      radical educational thinker,
      70, 71, 99
Hort, Fenton (1828–1892)
   Cambridge theologian, 38

132   INDEX

M

Mallock, William Hurrell
(1849–1923), 85
his *New Republic* (1877), 85
Manchester, 18, 20, 64, 65, 69
Martineau, James, vi, 4, 24–26,
28, 29, 31, 37, 42, 43, 47, 53, 55,
59, 69, 71, 80–84, 86,
101–106, 104n3
advocacy of an agent-based virtue
ethics, in opposition to
Sidgwick, 104
awareness of Maurice's failings as a
commentator on Coleridge, 81
centrality of his essay, 31
Greswell's uncertainty as to where
the essay was published, 20
his intellectual development closely
followed Coleridge's, but
differed in insisting on ultimately
rational conclusions, 81
Mary Anne Evans, 40, 71
Mill, John Stuart (1806–1873), 36, 84
radical philosopher, 84
Molteno, Percy Alport (1861–1937),
88, 88n1
sent Greswell his book on *Federal
South Africa* (1896), with
which Greswell did not
agree, 88
Mozley, John Rickards (1840–1931),
4, 24–26, 28, 31, 32, 43, 57, 69,
73, 81–84, 100, 106
his essay on Coleridge as a poet, 24,
43, 57, 84, 106
a nephew and correspondent of
John Henry and Francis Henry
Newman, 31
one of a trio of English radicals
whose essays Greswell appears
to have priviledged, 4
a prominent member of advanced
Cambridge circles (Grote Club
etc.), 31, 83

N

Newman, Francis William
(1805–1897), 31, 83, 122–123
brother of John Henry; uncle and
correspondent of John Rickards
Mozely, 31
contributes to *Westminster
Review*, 40
Newman, John Henry (1801–1890),
31, 81, 83
brother of John Henry; uncle and
correspondent of John
Rickards Mozely
first-named Coleridgean in
Martineau's essay, 26, 81
Pater's essay appeared when
Newman appeared old hat, 110
Nichols, William Luke (1802–1889),
58, 60, 93
retired priest, antiquary and author
at Stowey, 58, 60, 93

P

Pater, Walter (1839–1894), 4, 25, 26,
41, 43, 68, 69, 71, 82–85, 98,
105, 106
ambiguity of his original Coleridge
essay, 55, 68, 82
attraction for Greswell, 71, 83
choice of Allsop on which to found
his essay, 82
markings, 26
one of Greswell's three privileged
essays, 4, 83
published in Westminster Review, 41
revised, 55
Periodicals, v, 15, 17, 24, 38–41, 66, 76
See also Greswell's Coleridge
Workbook
Priestley, Joseph (1733–1804), 80
at beginnings of British
Unitarianism 180–81, 80
librarian at Calne, 80

INDEX   **133**

Q

The Quantocks area
  Greswell's later preference for East
    Somerset, 74, 91
  their then-recent discovery by
    "visitors", 57–60, 93–94

R

Rosehill Circle, Coventry
  low standing of Coleridge in, 78

S

Seeley, Sir John Robert (1834–1895),
    4, 5, 37, 69, 71, 81, 83–86, 89,
    97, 99–102
  anonymous author of contentious
    Ecce Homo (1865) and
    Natural Religion (1882), 4, 37,
    69, 83, 85, 86, 99
  elected Regius Professor of Modern
    History at Cambridge,
    1869–95, and author of the
    vastly popular Expansion of
    England (1883), 5, 71, 89
  influence of Seeley's colonial
    ideas on Greswell's Prize
    Essay, 89
  influential member of Cambridge
    group of intellectuals, 83
  James Martineau critical of natural
    religion, 102
Shrewsbury
  Coleridge's withdrawal from the
    Shrewsbury meeting noticed,
    43, 55, 77, 80
Sidgwick, Henry (1838–1900), 69,
    81, 83, 102–104
  member of distinctive Cambridge
    group (Seeley, Mozley,
    etc), 69, 83

The Methods of Ethics (1874)
  opposed by James Martineau in
    his *Types of Ethical Theory*
    (1885), 102
South Africa
  changing situation in, 74, 88
  and colonial federation, 3, 88
  Dutch and Germans in, 73, 89
  Greswell best at writing on fauna
    and flora of, 89
  teaching Kafirs, 73
  time taken to travel there, 90
  Westminster incompetence in
    dealing with, 74
  See also Frere, Sir Henry Bartle
    (1815–1884)
Stegmann, Rev. George William
  Bartle Frere's loyal Dutch secretary,
    112, 115, 123
Stowey, Nether, 3, 4, 43, 48, 58
  Coleridge cottage compared with
    Wordsworth's Dove
    Cottage, 92–94
  Greswell's activity to acquire the
    Coleridge Cottage for nation,
    3, 5, 61
  Greswell's greater interest in making
    it a local library, 5
  Greswell's writing on Nether
    Stowey, 92
  long-time lack of local interest in
    celebrating Coleridge, 43, 92
Strauss, David Friedrich
    (1808–1874), 78
  author of *Das Leben Jesu*
    (1835–36), 78

T

Tulloch, John (1823–1886), 37, 54, 98
  a narrower focus than Greswell's
    compilation, 37, 54, 98

U

University of Oxford's silent presence
  versus Cambridge intellectuals
    during nineteenth century, 83
  the Greswell family presence, 67,
    69, 73, 99
  Greswell's avoidance of Arnold,
    Jowett and the Balliol
    circle, 68, 71
  Pater's contentious position,
    4, 41, 55, 68

V

Virtue ethics
  agent-based, 104
  Coleridge's Remorse as classic
    illustration, 103
  James Martineau's championship, in
    dialogue with James
    Sidgwick, 103
  recent revival of interest in, 104n3

W

Ward, Mary Augusta (1851–1920)
  Greswell's tutor's wife, neice
    of Matthew Arnold, and
    author of *Robert Elsmere*
    (1888), 37–38, 68,
    97, 124
Wordsworth, John (1843–1911),
    38, 58, 68
  fellow of Brasenose, 1867–1883;
    Bampton Lecturer in
    1881, 37, 68
Wordsworth, William
    (1770–1850), 83, 89, 92–94,
    100, 102
  as Greswell's strong Stowey
    poet, 58, 89
  immediate popularity of Dove
    Cottage and cultural
    tourism, 93, 94
  Mozley's critique, 43, 83
  quoted, 100